To Love & To Cherish

To Love &

BRIDES REMEMBERED

LINDA OTTO LIPSETT

To Cherish

THE QUILT DIGEST PRESS   SAN FRANCISCO

Editorial and production direction by Michael M. Kile.
Editing by Harold Nadel.
Design by Kajun Graphics, San Francisco.
Most color photography by Sharon Risedorph, San Francisco.
Quiltmaking patterns and instructions by Laura Nownes.
Typesetting by Rock & Jones, Oakland, California.
Printed by Nissha Printing Company, Ltd., Kyoto, Japan.
Color separations by the printer.

Special thanks to:
Melissa Leventon, Nancy Cook and the Textile Department of The
Fine Arts Museums of San Francisco, for their very generous
support of this project.
Julie Silber for invaluable manuscript review.
Michael Greenwell and Michael Humphrey for the use of their home
to photograph the cover.
The Reverend Lesley Wilder for his assistance with the cover
photograph.
Irene Newmark.

First edition.
First printing.

Library of Congress Cataloging-in-Publication Data

Lipsett, Linda Otto, 1947–
    To love & to cherish.

    Bibliography: p.
    1. Marriage customs and rites — United States.
2. United States — Social life and customs — 19th
century. 3. Album quilts — United States. 4. Friendship
quilts — United States. I. Title. II. Title: To love
and to cherish.
GT2703.L57   1989   392'.5   89-10404
ISBN 0-913327-19-0
ISBN 0-913327-18-2

The Quilt Digest Press
955 Fourteenth Street
San Francisco 94114

For Harold and Ethel,
Whose marriage defines true love,
Whose lives together impart hope and inspiration.

Ethel Golden and Harold Nichols in their sixty-seventh year of marriage.

ACKNOWLEDGMENTS

I have truly enjoyed making exciting discoveries of the written word in diaries, letters, records, newspapers and books; but my greatest joys and lasting memories come from the wonderful friends who have helped me along the way: Robert E. and Miriam J. Higgins brought Harriet Higgins's family and story to life, introducing me to homesteading in Colorado in the 1890's. Ada Taylor's grandchildren John A. Dunsmoor, Henry L. Merritt and Rebecca Garland have generously shared their letters, diaries, photographs, Bible records and quilts with me so that Ada and Alva's loving marriage can be told. Then there are my dear friends Sherman and Norma Young, who took time from their dairy farm to show me the quaint hamlet of Abbotts Corner, Quebec. Norma also has spent hours and hours researching and copying Canadian records for me, invaluable in my search for the story of Cynthia Abbott Miner's friendship quilt. Dorothy and Arthur Pickard shared their Rockwell family collection with me and then did my leg work thousands of miles away, copying numerous pages of Rockwell letters that I desperately needed. Dear Florence J. Herrick, thanks to Richard Whitcomb's research and hand-drawn map, guided me to a forgotten cemetery on a pine-shrouded hillside overlooking the Connecticut River. Without Ina C. Adams, the story of the bridal friendship quilt of "Mrs. M" (Mary Mather Steel) would ever have remained a mystery. Two Ethels in the Mansfield, Connecticut area gave me Lucinda Place Howard's story: Ethel Larkin discovered the quiltmaker's ninety-two-year-old granddaughter Ethel Golden Nichols and helped me in so many other ways with research; Ethel Nichols told me about her grandmother Lucinda during many delightful, life-memorable conversations.

Ben and Lisa Bishop, Laurice and Bessie Wright, Serena J. May, Elizabeth Graham, Robert and Carol McHugh and Michael Perry warmly opened their historic stone and clapboard homes to me. In the process of restoring their early clapboard home, the Bishops even removed and gave me an historic piece of wallpaper still in the entry way since the 1860's, when Lucinda Place Howard had lived there.

So many wonderful people graciously stopped what they were doing to take me on incredible tours reconstructing the past: Orson G. Smith in Hinsdale, New Hampshire; Ethel Larkin, Mansfield, Connecticut; Edith Hunter through Weathersfield, Vermont; Charles Nelson and Ann Elizabeth Pardee to Hinsdale cemeteries; Elizabeth Graham and Nancy Evelyn Hall in the Hartland, Vermont area; and Mary B. Fenn through the West Windsor countryside.

Then there were so many who generously shared their expertise, memories and genealogy with me: Barbara Chiolino, Elizabeth Bailey, Virginia Butterfield, Richard Whitcomb, Roberta Smith, Russell Slate, Eleanor S. Smith, Kenneth Higgins, Phyllis Delano, Carol Pegalotti, Florence Powers, Erline Nixon, Virginia O'Neil, Elizabeth Spear, Carmine Guicca, Mr. and Mrs. Harry F. Olney, Marion Dana Hastings, Beatrice Cushman Dana, Clara L. Richardson, Lori Smith, Mildred Kittredge, Lillian Hatch Marcotte, Elizabeth Gillingham, Mrs. Frank Greene, Mrs. Theras Jenkins, Art Cohen, Mary Margaret Allard, Kay Muir, Doris Lucille Hibbard Jenkins, David M. Bell, Kathleen Bone, Dan Fenton, Vie N. Nash, Bunny Beard, Annette Mongeon, Yoshiye Sato Tsuboi, Masaye S. Kato, Roland Kato and Allen L. Stratton.

This book would not have been possible without the help of many knowledgeable and organized persons at museums, libraries and historical societies across the continent: Edith Hunter, Weathersfield (Vermont) Historical Society; Mary B. Fenn, West Windsor (Vermont) Historical Society; Alice Bayles, Dover (Vermont) Free Library; New Hampshire Historical Society; Pamela J. Cartledge, Connecticut Historical Society; Jeffrey Mayer, University of Connecticut; The Mansfield (Connecticut) Historical Society; Polly Mitchell, Shelburne Museum; Nancy A. Heywood, Essex Institute; Anne A. Salter, Atlanta Historical Society; Suzanne J. Stone, Westfield (Massachusetts) Athenaeum; Deborah Shelton, Arizona Historical Society; Debbie Mastel, San Joaquin County Historical Society, Lodi, California; Kathryn Otto and Nicolette Bromberg, The University of Kansas; Beverly Olmsted, New York State Historical Association; Tod Ruhstaller, The Haggin Museum; Fritz Hamer, South Carolina State Museum; Jessica Nicoll, Teresa Percy and Joan Allen, Old Sturbridge Village; Hood Museum of Art, Dartmouth College; Ruth Levin, The Bennington (Vermont) Museum; Jude Solomon, The Historic New Orleans Collection; Jeana Elizabeth Brunson, Museum of

Florida History; Barbara D. Hall, Hagley Museum and Library; Laura S. Cox, Maryland Historical Society; Elaine Owens, Mississippi Department of Archives and History; Elva B. Crawford and Diane Berger, National Society Daughters of The American Revolution; Ann Michele Poulos, Florida Museum of Natural History; Jan Heister and Kathryn Gaillard, The Charleston Museum; Marion Phelps, Brome County Historical Society, Quebec, Canada; Laura Holt, Laboratory of Anthropology, Museum of Indian Arts and Culture, Museum of New Mexico; Palace of the Governors, Museum of New Mexico; Dr. Andrea Shaw, Amherst (New York) Museum; Dr. Cora Norman, Mississippi Humanities Council; Susan Swan, The Henry Francis du Pont Winterthur Museum; Otto Thieme, Cincinnati Art Museum; Nancy Rexford, past curator of North Hampton (Massachusetts) Historical Society; Barbara D. Fiddler, Johnson (Vermont) State College.

My special thanks to my dearest friend, Charlotte Rau Ekback, for her brilliant ideas, invaluable advice and much-appreciated understanding.

And thanks to my family who have helped me in all aspects of this book: Marjorie Cooley; Bill and Sandy Otto; Michael Otto, my personal Civil War historian; Helen C. Lipsett for her exciting library finds; my grandmother Esther Rose Price for her rich memories and great wisdom. And love to my mother, Eileen Kelley, for the many precious hours we shared together on research trips. Finally thanks to my son, Robert, for his great patience on our trips. I hope someday he will think of the times we shared, if not with joy, at least with a smile!

Linda Otto Lipsett
Los Angeles
May 1989

CONTENTS

INTRODUCTION

I will never forget standing outside my grandmother's candy store in Dayton, Ohio, tears in my eyes, hugging everyone, saying good-byes. I was a new bride of twenty, headed for some dismal second-floor apartment in Illinois. Always will I remember the last words urgently shouted to me as I was getting into the car. My mother said, "Don't forget to clean the toilets every day"; my grandmother, "Don't put tomato paste in your iron skillet." With that advice I was off to begin my married life.

I wonder now what Ellen Spaulding Reed's mother told her in 1854 as she was boarding the train for a tiny log house in Wisconsin. Or what advice Nancy Place gave her daughter Lucinda, packing for her husband's family's farmhouse in Providence, Rhode Island. Or Rhoda Peck Fisher to Harriet Fisher Higgins, climbing into the wagon about to leave New Hampshire for a log house in a new settlement high up in the Green Mountains. Doubtless, those last words from Mother were similar — useful instruction after all the loving farewells, for each mother wanted her daughter's marriage to be *successful,* that she be a good wife for her husband first. Then all else would follow.

For twenty-one years, I have heard my mother's and grandmother's voices in my head. *Never* do I put tomato paste in my black skillet. The toilets? — Oh, well . . .

Linda Otto Lipsett
Los Angeles
May 1989

Ethel Golden (also see cover and pages 81 and 99) at the time she was engaged to Harold Nichols.
Photograph courtesy of Ethel Golden Nichols.

I have won the love of one of the best men I ever met.
Oh! life seems so bright and happy to me now,
and the future seems much brighter.[1]

Love was the inspiration, marriage the bond that settled America and pushed the young nation predictably westward. It was love and promises that took a bride away from home, family, the mill or schoolhouse, perhaps forever, to follow after her husband or intended into the virgin wilderness, onto vast prairies, or to some far-removed outpost for better, for worse, for richer, for poorer. And it was love that gave her the hope, intensity and energy to go about her mundane drudgery, day in and day out, working for a better future. She was doing these tasks for her husband, for her family, for her home. Ultimately, however, it was not love but the commitment of marriage that *kept* the woman there despite hardships, loneliness, disease and personal tragedy.

For every married woman across nineteenth-century America, her wedding was the most significant event of her life. In those few moments, no matter how elegant or humble the surroundings, whether in her parents' home, in a church, at the justice of the peace or in only a shift on the King's Highway, she permanently committed herself to the man standing there at her side clasping her hand. Before God and witnesses, she promised to be this man's helpmeet, to bear and raise his children, to make his home, to work alongside him for as long as they both should live.

It was only natural then that a woman took "the great state of matrimony"[2] very seriously. "My whole being is pervaded by a kind of serious strain of thought.... This getting married is no trifle, but a event that gives use to grave serious thought," wrote one young woman the morning of her wedding. For her, marriage meant "the crowning glory of woman's life this giving up herself to the one who is her glory."[3] For Lavina Thomas Gates the emotional strain was too much. The wedding ceremony was to be at 2 o'clock the next afternoon, yet Lavina only penned into her diary, "Felt very poorly Headache — ."[4]

Lavina was not alone. Across America as their wedding days approached, brides-to-be had mixed emotions — they were nervous and scared, excited and happy: understandably so, for the typical woman's wedding was not only the most significant event, it was also the highpoint in her life. She had most likely dreamed of that day since she was only a girl. It was as if that day was snatched out of time, hers alone. For those few fleeting, enchanting moments, she was the center of attention. Around *her* everything else revolved. No matter what her life was to bring later — no matter the thousands of dirty dishes and wash basins slopping over in lye water; childbirth, squalling babies, diapers, and sickness; no matter that her hands were now etched and scarred, worn hard and rough from the years of toil — she would always have those cherished memories of her wedding day.

Surprisingly, she kept those memories to herself. The nineteenth-century woman seldom, if ever, discussed such personal subjects as her wedding. Her own daughters probably knew little about that most important day in their mother's life. Her wedding, her dress, the preparations, her emotion, she kept to herself. Her wedding gown might have been carefully folded and preserved in a trunk somewhere, someday to be discovered and valued *if* it was a traditional white gown. If it were expensive enough, it might be proudly donated to a museum. But if the bride had worn instead only her colorful best dress, the dress was most likely passed over, even discarded during the years. It was not stunning enough for a granddaughter to donate to a museum. Who should ever be interested in a common, country girl's best dress? Only the breathtaking white creations of the well-to-do in the cities were thought worthy of preservation. Besides, those gowns were *obviously* wedding gowns; only the bride herself knew that the frayed, worn, striped, blue-brown silk with the fringe-trimmed bell sleeves and skirt ten yards around was the dress she had worn for her wedding so many years earlier.

"The bride wore white" and she lived happily ever after: that was most young women's dream, but over time that dream became "remembered" reality. The wedding dress of the country bride was forgotten, as was her steadfast marriage of strength, courage and devotion.

An old woman with her spinning wheel, c. 1900. *Collection of the author.*
Spinning was one of the most important skills of American women throughout the first quarter of the nineteenth century and continuing much later in poorer and western frontier areas. A woman's ability to provide the thread and yarn for clothing and bedding made her indispensable for a man: it was an integral part of her worth to him.
Spinning was resumed again in the hard times during the Civil War. In Wisconsin in 1864, Willard Reed wrote, "we made 25 yds. of flanel last fall, and are agoing to make some linen this summer. we got along without buying much, you know it does not cost much to support pride here." (*From a letter by J. W. Reed to his in-laws Arterista and Stedman Spaulding, March 27, 1864. Courtesy of Barbara Chiolino.*)

When Nancy Barnard Batchelder was a little girl, in the 1820's, her first "'stent' was one skein of tow and this was increased as [she] grew taller and stronger." Later on, provided that someone carded for her, "six skeins were a day's work."[5] By the time Nancy reached her teenage years, she should be able to card *and* spin four skeins a day, the same as her mother did daily.

When there was "enough tow for a web of twenty yards, it was boiled out in ashes and water and well washed to soften it, then spooled and warped ready to weave into cloth."[5] In those years (the first part of the nineteenth century), all the cloth Nancy's family used or wore was made from the tow or wool she and her mother and sisters had spun and woven.

In truth, Nancy and her sisters were "spinsters." All unmarried girls at that time were referred to as spinsters, having to spin enough bedding and linen so that they were well prepared for their households after marriage.[6] "At that time, no young lady would think of getting married until she had spun and woven cloth sufficient for her sheets and table cloths, and had filled a pillow-bier with stockings of her own knitting." "One young lady, after filling a pillow-bier with stockings for herself, actually knit a quantity of different sizes for her future husband, should she ever meet with an individual to bear the name; and notwithstanding it was generally known, not one of the ungrateful sex would ever propose."[7]

When Bessie, a poor minister's daughter in New England, was engaged to be married, "she was obliged to defer the wedding, for she had made no preparation for such an event. Could her own spinning have been reserved for future use, as was the custom with other young ladies at the time, she would have had an ample supply of all necessary articles for such an occasion. But all her's [sic] had been used to supply the immediate wants of the family; and instead of having a pillow-bier filled with stockings, she had not one of her own to fill." But she was well prepared and could quickly make enough. "In about six months after her engagement to be married, her articles were all complete for house-keeping."[8]

Across America, "spinster" early on became a woman ridiculed. From Colonial times, an "antient maid" or spinster was twenty-five, and a "thornback"[9] thirty. With a majority of men, there were few old maids, and the possibility of being one was almost unthinkable. In Virginia, "an Old Maid or an Old Bachelor [was] as scarce . . . and reckoned as ominous as a Blazing Star."[10] In complimenting one old maid, one man wrote, "An *old* (or Superannuated) Maid in Boston is thought such a curse, as nothing can exceed it (and looked on as a *dismal* spectacle). . . . She is now about thirty years. . . . Yet she never disguises herself, and talks as little as she thinks of love."[11]

Despite her careful preparations for marriage, Nancy Batchelder had cause to be alarmed. She had watched each of her sisters wed. School terms had passed one into the next for her as school mistress. It was not until she was twenty-five, on the evening of March 12, 1840, that she was finally married at her father's house, "the room . . . lighted by a bright fire in the fireplace and tallow candles."[12]

There simply was no alternative to marriage. Spinsters were rare and usually to be pitied, especially through the first half of the nineteenth century.

Ethel Golden (photo on page 16) first knew Harold Nichols in high school, but then she thought him "such a pest. He always wanted to talk to me about what the boys were doing. I didn't care what the boys were doing. I didn't care about boys, period." In 1915, Harold came over to her church. "I tried to get him signed up for new members, and every time I started up to him, he was out the door. I asked my mother if I could call him up. She said that under the circumstances I could. So I called him up and asked him if he would join. He said he would, and I asked him 'When?' He said 'Sunday,' and I said, 'Would you wait for me?'"
Nothing more had come of their friendship until the United States entered World War I. On June 6, 1917, Harold enlisted as an electrician with the Navy. Word reached his "chums" in Connecticut that Harold was lonely and homesick. They suggested that Ethel write to him to cheer him up. "I had the nerve to write him first," Ethel remarked, adding with a sparkling smile, "Harold wrote back immediately. . . . From the first letter, I fixed him. At first we wrote two or three times a week, then every day. Eleven months after I started writing, we were engaged." Harold recalled this photograph with a romantic twinkle in his eye at age 92, "I liked *that* one. She was a pretty good-looking girl!"

Under most circumstances they would never have privacy and a home of their own but always have to live at the mercy of others. Spinsters, as well as bachelors, were especially frowned upon in Colonial times. At first, unmarried women had been given their own parcels of land, but an end was soon put to that. "It would be a bad president [sic]...to keep hous [sic] alone,"[13] the Massachusetts governor told Deborah Holmes as a reason for not allowing her land ownership. In New Haven the early law read:

Single persons, not in service or dwelling with their relatives are forbidden to diet or lodge alone; but they are required to live in "licensed" families; and the governors of such families are ordered to observe the course, carriage, and behavior of every such single person, whether he or she walk diligently in a constant lawful employment, attending both family duties and the public worship of God, and keeping good order day and night or otherwise.[14]

Even into the nineteenth century, it was customary that a single woman should live with family; she had little possibility of earning enough money to support herself comfortably. Schoolteaching was the most common profession for an unmarried woman, but that job paid her only half or less of what the schoolmaster received, and summer and winter school terms made up only a part of the year.

Of course, a spinster could look upon herself as a failure in woman's most important role: childbearing. A good woman had children and many of them. A spinster or barren wife had difficulty fitting into society. She was different from the rest, sharing little in common with the exhausted married women discussing their last lying in, mourning a child's death, or bragging over the pantaloons they were making for their little girls. Especially on the western frontier, women without children were often excluded, maybe not intentionally, but childbirth, children, courtships and marriages were important topics of conversation. Spinsters and childless women found themselves left out of the conversation around the frame at the neighbor's big quilting. Twenty-year-old Ellen Spaulding Reed, even though married, was homesick and lonely way out west in Burke, Wisconsin. She had had no children and made the excuse "Babies are as thick out here as flies in the sumer [sic], but poor folks like us cannot afford it."[15] Still Ellen could continue to *try* to have a child; with the passing of the years, an unmarried woman's outlook became all the more hopeless and bleak.

Childless married women also had the option and many times easy opportunity to adopt or raise someone else's child. Sadly, with the thousands and thousands of families suddenly packing up and moving to some unknown wilderness or inhospitable environment, many children were left with family members or friends back home or somewhere along the way, maybe never to be claimed again. Ellen Spaulding Reed was so happy when she wrote home, "Perhaps you did not know we have got a little girl at our house, well we have, and one that is not to be sneered at too. . . . our girl is one that we have taken if her mother dont come and take her and she is in California so there is not much danger   she is 8 years old and her mother is sister to George Spauldings wife."[16]

A teacher with her scholars, on the porch of Mossdale School, California. *Collection of the author.*

With the threat of having their daughters end up spinsters, mothers had to depend upon advice from a variety of sources. Unfortunately, most of the printed word was written by men. The newspapers were always generous with tips for women as to the qualifications that made a good wife. Not appearance, not finery, but work and productivity were what won a man's affections: "ninety-nine hundredths of all the finery with which women decorate, or load their persons, go for nothing, as far as husband-catching is concerned — Where and how, then, do men find their wives? — In the quiet homes of their parents or guardians — at the fireside, where the domestic graces and feelings are alone domesticated. These are the charms which most surely attract the high as well as the humble."[17]

Of course, the more productive a woman was, including bearing children, the better. And she was reminded often by neighbors, gossip or newspapers and periodicals of the feats of other married women which she should strive to live up to. Sometimes she was even dared: "Young Ladies, Beat This If You Can" certainly caught her eye as she scanned the newspaper. "In the town of Williamsburgh, Mass., resides Mrs Aaron Warner, a lady of 75 years of age. During the summer of 1848, she spun 100 runs of woolen yarn; doubled and twisted 45 runs of it; knit 76 pair of men's seamed socks, and wove 60 yards of rug carpeting, besides doing the ordinary housework for her family. The past summer she has made four hundred weight of most excellent cheese; wove more than twenty-five yards of flannel; spun and doubled and twisted yarn for sixty pairs of men's socks, besides doing many other kinds of work. She is a perfect pattern of order, neatness and industry, and furnishes an example that all yonger [sic] ladies would do well to imitate."[18]

Ada C. Taylor Dunsmoor actually knew an amazingly productive woman like this near the old stone house in West Windsor, Vermont. She would tell her own children one day of the "industrious housewife who requested her husband to walk the horse to church so she could knit."[19]

Over and over again, mothers were warned that their "Daughters should thoroughly acquaint themselves with the business and cares of a family. These are among the first objects, of a woman's creation.... They should learn neatness, economy, industry and sobriety. These will constitute their ornaments."[20]

One stereoscopic image of a little girl mending her doll, c. 1900. *Collection of the author.*
"Through their dolls, 'little mothers' began to gain basic sewing skills as well as a sense of what society would expect from them as women. This socialization, achieved through needlework training, was passed on from mother (or aunt or grandmother) to daughter generation to generation, in a continuous female legacy." (Pat Ferrero, Elaine Hedges and Julie Silber, *Hearts and Hands* [San Francisco: The Quilt Digest Press, 1987], p. 19.)

But not only men wrote of the necessary qualities for wives; women writers often mimicked them, worrying women with their stern, foreboding words: "a thorough, religious, *useful* education is the best security against misfortune, disgrace and poverty. . . . Young ladies should be taught that usefulness is happiness, and that all other things are but incidental."[21]

With all the severity in their lives, women often times found great relief in *Godey's*, the most important and widely circulated periodical of the mid-nineteenth century.[22] Its brilliant editor, Sarah J. Hale, meant only to humor her ladies when she printed "MAXIMS" in the May 1867 magazine: "A good wife should be like three things, which three things she should not be like. She should be like a town-clock, keep time and regularity; she should not be like a town-clock, speak so loud that all the town may hear. She should be like an echo, speak when she is spoken to; she should not be like an echo, always to have the last word. She should be like a snail, keep within her own house; she should not be like a snail, carry all she has upon her back."[23]

Of course, practical instruction on getting a man was always appreciated. Found among the papers of a "late dowager" was "Advice to Unmarried Ladies." Perhaps the widow had followed this same advice as a young woman, with good results:

If you have blue eyes — languish.
If black eyes — leer.
If you have pretty feet — wear short petticoats.
If you are the least *doubtful* as to that point — let them be rather long.
If you have good teeth — don't forget to laugh now and then.
If you have bad ones — you must only simper.
While you are young — sit with your face to the light.
When you are a little advanced — sit with your back to the window.
If you have a bad voice — always speak in a low tone.
If it is acknowledged that you have a fine voice — never speak in a high tone.
If you dance well — dance but seldom.
If you dance ill — never dance at all.
If you sing well — make no previous excuses.
If you sing indifferently — hesitate not a moment when you are asked, for few persons are competent judges of singing, but every one is sensible of a desire to please.
If you wish to let the world know you are in love with a particular man — treat him with formality, and every one else with ease and freedom.
If you are disposed to be pettish or insolent — it is better to exercise your ill humour on your dog, your cat, or your servant, than your friends.[24]

Despite male dominance in all aspects of their lives, women retaliated in their own clever ways. With humor and sarcasm they made up their own criteria for good men. "How to Pick a Husband — 1850" had this to say:

If a man wipes his feet on the door-mat, he will make a good domestic husband. If a man in snuffing a candle puts it out, you may be sure he will make a stupid husband. If a man puts his handkerchief on his knee while taking tea, you may be sure he will be a prudent husband. The man who wears rubbers and is careful about wrapping himself up before venturing in the night air not unfrequently makes a good invalid husband, that mostly stops at home, and is easily comforted with slops.[25] The man who watches the kettle, and prevents its boiling over, will not fail in his married state in exercising the same care in always keeping the pot boiling. The man who does not take tea, ill-treats the cat, takes snuff, stands with his back to the fire, is a brute whom I would advise you not to marry upon any circumstances, either for love or money — but most decidedly not for love.[26]

It was a well-known fact that, in spite of all men might say about women, they needed them for their very well-being. Even Voltaire was quoted in *Godey's* as saying, "The more married men you have the fewer crimes there will be. Marriage renders a man more virtuous and more wise. An unmarried man is but half of a perfect being, and it requires the other half to make things right; and it cannot be expected that in this imperfect state he can keep the straight path of rectitude any more than a boat with one oar, or a bird with one wing, can keep a straight course."[27]

There were many women, like twenty-year-old Jemima Condict, eighteen-year-old Eliza Southgate, and twenty-six-year-old Eleanor Cohen Seixas, who believed "it was better to be married than single, but better to be single than unhappily wed."[28] After all, marriage was forever; separation could not even be considered as an alternative.

At twenty, Jemima Condict in West Orange, New Jersey, wrote into her diary how she scared Mr. Chandler off. When he had asked her why she did not marry, she had answered that she "want in no hurry." When he told her he wished he was married to her, she answered that "he would Soon wish himself on maried agin" because she was "a crose ill contrived Pese of Stuf." Jemima wrote on, "I told him that I would advise all the men to remain as they was for the women was Bad & the men so much worse that It was a wonder if they agreed."[29] Actually, Jemima had a reason for her actions: she was in love with her cousin. Although cousins were a commonplace couple throughout the mid-nineteenth century, there was controversy as to whether that relationship was right or wrong, just as there had been for decades as to the religious and moral ethics of marrying one's deceased wife's sister.

In Maine, Eliza Southgate wrote, "I could never love without being beloved, and I am confident in my own mind that no person whom I could love would ever think me sufficiently worthy to love me. But I congratulate myself that I am at liberty to refuse those I don't like, and that I have firmness enough to brave the sneers of the world and live an old maid, if I never find one I can love."[30]

Considering herself a spinster, Eleanor Cohen (Seixas) of Columbia, South Carolina, had written into her diary, "At sixteen I fancied if I was unmarried at 25, I would surely be an old maid and feel inclined to resign all gayety, now I have reached 26, I feel nearly as young I did then, and wonder, if it is possibly true, that I am so old. . . . I have had several beaux and love affairs,

and was privately engaged to be married at sixteen to one I thought the perfection, of a man, now with increased years, and maturity of judgment I bless God I did not marry him, I am quick tempered, but warm and loving he is jealous, passionate, dictatorial, and harsh, and had I married him, my life would have been an endless quarrel, or I would have sunk into being a slave! But God kindly spared me, and tho at the time I suffered, as every woman must, when she sees her idol shattered, yet I now, and have for years blessed God, that I did not marry my 'first love.'"[31]

At twenty-two and courting Abraham Lincoln, Mary Todd wrote to her friend that she had "caught a glimpse" of Miss Lamb, and that she "looked becomingly happy at the prospect" of getting married the next week. Then Mary went on to say, "I am pleased she is about perpetrating the crime of matrimony, like some of our friends in this place." But concerning another new bride, Mary wrote, Mrs. Abell's "silver tones, the other evening were not quite so captain like as was their wont in former times, why is it that married folks always become so serious?"[32]

Some persons actually had the temerity publicly to defy the prejudices of spinsterhood in articles such as "Old Maids":

We wish that something could be done to cure the terrible dread which young girls under twenty have of being "old maids," for then there would be a far larger number of happy wives than there now are. We verily and verily believe that many of the unhappy matches which curse mankind, are the result of this dread. Young girls seem to think that if they are not married at twenty, they shall lose caste; and hence, accept the first offer they have, without duly weighing the consequences. Mistaken souls! it were infinitely better that they were never married than that they should be mis-married.

Among the foolish prejudices, which discredit the judgment of mankind, the prejudice against old maids is one of the most foolish. The very fact that a lady is an old maid, is, or ought to be, creditable. It is an evidence that she possesses prudence, forethought and a refined taste — admirable qualities in a woman. The old maid generally has the virtue of prudence in its perfection; she has had offers of marriage; no doubt, what lady of thirty and upwards has not? She has rejected several suitors, and doubtless she has reasons for so doing. Much better is it to be a happy old maid than a miserable wife. [33]

Lithograph entitled "Divided Attention," *Godey's Lady's Book and Magazine,* September 1867, p. 197.

Nevertheless, women looked forward to the stories and poems on romance, brides and weddings that appeared often in the popular periodicals. In February of 1856, thousands of that month's *Godey's* were mailed out across the states and territories of the country. By the light of crackling hearths and bursting pitch-pine knots, tallow candles or whale-oil lamps, women excitedly opened their new magazines and escaped from the dark, dreary walls of logs and chinking, or sod and rough plaster. Unmarried girls dreamed of their own future weddings; married women remembered that glorious moment when their futures had appeared so bright and happy. There were also men subscribing to *Godey's*, who read their copies hoping for clues and advice on marriage for the objects of their attention. One man had "a little lady-love in the country to whom [he] always [sent] the 'Book' after having read it and marked various pieces for her particular attention."[34] Perhaps he hoped she would think of him and marriage as she read "The Christmas Eve Bridal":

> She stands before the altar — one fair hand
> Clasped in her lover's — while an angel band,
> Unseen, this Christmas Eve, keeps watch above,
> To see her wear the crown of wedded love.
> Not purer the white veil that binds her hair;
> Not sweeter the sweet rose-buds nestling there,
> Than she, in maiden innocence and love,
> Trembling unto his bosom like a dove.
>
> The box and cedar round the chancel shine,
> In wreath and star, and festoon they entwine;
> Young Bride! methinks it is an omen sweet,
> The future bright as boughs your glances meet!
>
> Oh, love, young love! if but a *dream* thou art,
> It is the sweetest ever thrilled the heart!
> Love is no dream — they never felt its power
> Who call it but the sparkle of an hour —
> Love is no dream — it blooms, and never dies,
> It perfumes earth, its root is in the skies.[35]

The majority of young women reading this poem knew their own wedding would be different from this. It would most likely be not in a church but at home. In rural areas across the country, they would most probably not don fashionable white veils and wedding gowns specially made for those occasions either — that simply was not practical. Only girls from wealthy families could expect such bridal dresses. The country bride would wear the best dress she could, of the most fashionable cloth and style her family or she herself could provide. And she would not be ashamed, either, for that was very acceptable. All of her friends would do the same. There was one stanza of the poem that she did hope to have, however, and that was love, "the sweetest ever thrilled the heart," a love that bloomed and never died. That love, she was told, could be hers if she were careful to choose her husband

BRIDAL

The word bridal *came from a fund-raising custom in England in the sixteenth and seventeenth centuries in which the bride brewed a strong "bride-ale" to sell to her friends and neighbors. This was usually held immediately after the wedding ceremony. Everyone had plenty to drink, and then the collection box was passed around.*

well. But that was a problem in itself. Only during leap year were "unmarried ladies . . . privileged to pop the question to tardy swains and undeclared admirers";[36] otherwise, choice was the man's option. She could only refuse or accept a proposal. Ideally the man of her dreams would ask for her hand in real life and then they would certainly live happily forever after. "Leave the affections to nature and to truth, and all will end well," was *The Frugal Housewife*'s advice. Over and over women were warned of many unhappy wives who married simply "for the sake of the *name* of being married."[37]

In 1801 Eliza Southgate wrote to her cousin on the matter of choice:

> Every being who has contemplated human nature on a large scale will certainly justify me when I declare that the inequality of privilege between the sexes is very sensibly felt by us females, and in no instance is it greater than in the liberty of choosing a partner in marriage; true, we have the liberty of refusing those we don't like, but not of selecting those we do. . . . No woman, or rather not one in a hundred, married the man she should prefer to all the world — not that I ever could suppose

One stereoscopic image of young girls playing brides, c. 1900. *Collection of the author.*

that at the time she married him she did not prefer him to all others — but that she would have preferred another if he had professed to love her as well as the one she married.[38]

There were many young women like Jane Rockwell who were ashamed to admit to others of their unmarried status — that they were actually already maiden ladies, spinsters in the eyes of the community. Jane and her younger sister Ethelyn were so concerned "that they did not yet have husbands" that they "each bought a diamond ring and gave them to each other. If anyone asked where they got their new diamond, they very coyly said that someone had given it to them."[39]

Even when a young woman had a beau, courtships could be difficult; many times he would have to travel great distances to see her. With such large families, being alone with him was also difficult if not impossible. Certainly her sweetheart must not grow frustrated in his efforts to converse with her. Trying to court her at the hearth with her mother, father, brothers and sisters all there presented a real challenge. In the Connecticut Valley young lovers spoke to one another from opposite ends of the fireplace through a courting stick, a long hollow tube with mouth and earpieces.

These men may have traveled hours in frigid weather to see their intended on a Saturday night. It was not thrifty to keep a fire in the hearth after nine o'clock, and it was too great a distance for her beau to return home through the dangerous pitch-black night. There was little room for family members themselves within the crowded log or clapboard house. It seemed only sensible that, after the fire was put out, the couple be placed in bed with their clothing on, the "bundling" varying in degrees from a "very appropriate and secure night dress" with boards between them to actual one-legged dresses and knotted petticoats.

One man described his partner's attire in about 1829 not "like a bloomer . . . but something like a common dress, excepting the lower part, which is furnished with legs, like drawers properly attached. The dress is drawn at the neck and waist with strings tied with a very strong knot, and over this is put the ordinary apparel."[40] The couple would have privacy this way but were expected by their rigorous puritanical upbringings to act morally as their consciences dictated.

Bundling, or "bed fellowship,"[41] became a common practice in the countryside for poorer people in many northeastern states. There was much pressure on a young woman to bundle; she knew if she refused she might possibly lose her beau altogether. And, even worse, she would be made a laughing stock.

During the first quarter of the nineteenth century, bundling was so publicly ridiculed that it became a widespread embarrassment and disgrace. Bundling's final demise came when almanacs and broadsides held such verse as "A New Bundling Song," which was shockingly graphic for its time. The sarcasm was aimed at the female, not at her suitor:

"You don't undress, like man and wife,"
That is your plea, I'll freely own,
But whose [sic] your bondsmen when alone,
That further rules you will not break,
And marriage liberties partake?
Some really do, as I suppose,
Upon design keep on some clothes,
And yet in truth I'm not afraid
For to describe a bundling maid;
She'll sometimes say when she lies down,
She can't be cumber'd with a gown,
And that the weather is so warm,
To take it off can be no harm. . . .
But she is modest, also chaste,
While only bare from neck to waist,
And he of boasted freedom sings,
Of all above her apron strings.
Another pretty lass we'll scan,
That loves to bundle with a man,
For many different ways they take,
Through modest rules they all will break.
Some clothes I'll keep on, she will say,
For that has always been my way,
Nor would I be quite naked found,
With spark in bed, for thousand pound.
But petticoats, I've always said,
Were never made to wear in bed,
I'll take them off, keep on my gown,
And then I dare defy the town,
To charge me with immodesty,
While I so ever cautious be.[42]

Bundling did occasionally result in pregnancies, but it was argued by those who had courted in that way that "there wasn't any more mischief done those days than there is now."[43] Many argued that the newly invented sofa in use all year, especially in the summer, was far more dangerous than the old-fashioned featherbed for bundling only in winter. In fact, during and after the Revolution, pregnant brides were common: "Nearly one-third of rural New England's brides were already with child."[44] Babies born five to seven months after marriage were not unusual and were accepted in most communities.

Perhaps a woman suffered far less with shame because of a hurried marriage with her sweetheart than with worry that she might indeed be unable to bear him children at all. After all, she most likely was aware of the absolute necessity that she have children, especially boys. It would be a terrible burden both financially and physically on her future husband without sons to help farm his land. Pity the poor farmer who had to pay hired help year in

A bride must not finish dressing until the very last moment before leaving for church. For good luck, one last stitch should be put into her dress.

'Tis ill luck for a bride to see her face in a glass by candlelight.

A bride should not look in a mirror before she is dressed, nor after her toilet is completed.

It is unlucky to show the wedding gown before the wedding.

The bride and groom should not meet till the altar. (Victorian)

The trousseau should not be assembled before the eve of the wedding.

Linen should be marked with the bride's maiden name instead of her married name or initials. It is unwise for her to sign or be called her new name before it is officially hers. (Couples were even afraid to be photographed together before they were married.)

If you get married when the clock's hands are moving downward, your married life will go down also. If the hands are going upward, your marriage will be successful and happy.

Whistling around the wedding dress conjures up evil spirits.

Never tack the dress with black thread, which is associated with mourning.

A penny sewed into the seam of the bridal gown brings luck wherever it goes later.

Whoever sews the first stitch into the wedding gown will be married one year later.

Postponing a wedding day is bad luck.

A flight of birds as the bride goes to church on her wedding day means many children in the future.

and year out, instead of working strong boys of his own siring. It was not always by accident that a man got his intended pregnant. He could not chance the grave misfortune of marrying a barren woman; therefore, lucky was she who found herself with child and a need for a best dress and lots of wedding cake — in a hurry.

Times were changing, however. By 1830, the marrying age of women was between 22 and 26, instead of 19 to 23, as it was at the start of the nineteenth century.[45] With fewer child-bearing years during marriage, she could expect a family of five children, instead of the average eight of her mother's and grandmother's generations. By the 1840's, with radically reversed thoughts and published words on sex, along with Victorian, strait-laced morality, there were fewer and fewer girls pregnant before their marriages. Thought was to change so drastically from that of the early 1800's that those young women who had conceived out of wedlock found themselves ridiculed and ashamed. A woman simply had to be a virgin when she was married or she was not considered to be a good woman.

On the record, and even at the time, it looked as if Lucinda Place Howard had conceived her child before marriage: after all, the child was born only eight months after their wedding. Lucinda knew the truth, however. She had been forced to do regular farm work "just the same as the hired man. It was pretty heavy work lifting hay up and all, and she wasn't a very rugged person then." She worked so hard that she had nearly lost little Eugene. "He was born at seven months, without any fingernails or toenails, not even three pounds. He was so fragile and tiny at first that he couldn't even stand milk so Lucinda made a gruel out of oatmeal for him. She wasn't one to worry much, but for a couple of months, she wondered if he was going to pull through."[46]

Julia Stevens Crosby's son was born in 1818, only five months after her marriage to Orra; yet many years later his date of birth was changed on his gravestone to the following year. Was it not the new Victorian public condemnation that forced a permanent lie upon Julia's dear son's stone? No matter that others would not remember or know the date of her marriage; Julia herself did, and that was what mattered.

or many young women, finding a beau and courting was simple. Often a couple had lived near one another, maybe even on adjoining farms, attending the little one-room school together for many years. As a girl, Harriet Fisher had seen Oliver Higgins's silhouette against the New Hampshire horizon, helping his father plow the fields to the south of her father's farm. She had seen him driving the wagon to the mill or the village store down the dirt road, and she had recited in the one-room wooden school, a mile down the road, with Oliver Higgins, three years older and in another grade, seated in the same small room.

Thirty years of age, Ephraim Howard farmed with his father on the farm adjoining Lucinda Place's aunt and uncle, Isabel and Daniel Leonard, in Eastford, Connecticut. Daniel Leonard still lived there and was making

One stereoscopic image of a couple courting in a buggy, c. 1900, inscribed "Always Take a Horse You can Drive with One Hand."
Collection of the author.

קול ששון וקול שמחה, קול חתן וקול כלה.

MARRIAGES

Rabbi HIRSH BERMAN,

request the pleasure of your company at the marriage ceremony of his son

Samuel Berman to Annie Siegel,

on Sunday, December 22th, 1895, 5 P. M.,

at Standard Hall, Cor. Baltimore & Frederick St.

Bride's Residence, 210 S. Caroline Street.

Please bring this Invitation with you.

הורב צבי הירש בערמאן.

לאדעט זיא אונד איהרע ווערטהע פאמיליע איין צור האכ־
צייט פון זיין זאהן

שמואל מרדכי בערמאן מיט חנה רויזע סיגעל,
אם זאנטאג, דען 22טען דעצעמבער, 5 אוהר אבענד,
אין סטענדערט האלל, קאר. באלטימארע און פרעדעריק סט.
כלה'ס רעזידענץ, 210 סויטה קאראליי ן סטריט.
ביטטע דיעזען אינווייטישאן מיטצוברייגגען.

M. Silberman. N. 112 Printer. High St., Baltimore, Md.

Wedding invitation of Samuel Berman and Annie Siegel, Baltimore, Maryland. *Collection of the Maryland Historical Society, Baltimore.*

---

shoes, as he had when Lucinda's father had been there over thirty years earlier. The Leonards had always been close family to widowed Nancy Place and her girls. In fact, as a baby Lucinda had been given her middle name "Leonard" because of her parents' love for the family. It was only natural that Lucinda's friendship with her aunt and uncle's neighbor Ephraim Howard had grown into a most devoted love, and so, by 1851, the couple were making plans to be married.

In Vermont, Marion Dana Hastings first discovered her beau when she was picking blackberries with her friend. She reminisced, "The boys used to go and feed their sheep every morning." Then she added, with an impish giggle, "He used to come over through the woods to see me because he lived just over the hill."[47]

Having recently arrived from Virginia, Ethel Edmunds was dressed in her new green riding habit when she rode sidesaddle into the "raw western town" of Tucson in 1889 and met her future husband, Mose Drachman. After shopping, she had "sweetly asked the shy, ill-at-ease young man in front of Zeckendorf's store to help her back on her horse." As she remembered, "I was ready to mount and told him when I counted three I would jump and he was to hold my foot. Well, I jumped, but he just stood there and I went over the saddle, my arms hanging on one side and my feet on the other. My hat rolled in the sand. I was furious. 'Why didn't you hold my foot?' 'I never helped a lady on before.' 'You needn't tell me, I know it.'" She had ridden

The *Gleaner*, a sailing canal schooner owned by the Rockwell family. This was an odd type of sailing vessel in the United States, appearing on only a few bodies of water. *Photograph given to the author by Robert McHugh.*

away indignantly, but Mose "was intrigued," and enrolled in her dance class. Although inept at helping her onto a horse, he was actually a fine dancer. With persistence, he won Ethel's heart; in spite of the fact that she was not Jewish, they were married — although they had to run away to California to do so.[48]

Not all women were so fortunate as to see their sweethearts so often. With distances and travel lengthy, at times impossible, a young couple might have to rely on letters for long periods of time. In many rural areas, even in the more populated areas of the east, a lost letter could precipitate a broken heart or a misunderstanding that would end a romance. Even in times when roads, lakes and rivers were impassable, gossip had a way of reaching into the remote areas and frequently was the only communication a young lady would have to judge her beau's true intentions.

Lucy Ann McElroy's and Ell B. Rockwell's courtship had almost ended in 1855 as the result of a lost letter and untrue gossip. For Lucy it had seemed an eternity since that dreamy day in the summer when the dashing steamer pilot Ell and she had sat in the parlor and he had told her of his devotion for her alone. Then he had taken the canal boat up the Hudson through the locks at the Glens Falls feeder, headed for Lake Champlain. Lucy had waited for the mail, for a visit from her intended, but there was only silence. Then came the news she had feared most: destroying all of Lucy's hopes, her friend Emeline told her "of rumors of a certain young Lady"[49] with Ell.

Maybe Emeline had had her own personal intentions in later visiting Ell; nevertheless, it was only too fortunate for Lucy that Emeline actually talked to him in person. His letter of July 28th most likely had been lost somewhere between Port Henry and Sandy Hill, New York, and then he had become gravely ill in Whitchall, and in the care of "two young Ladies."[49] As it turned out, those months of Lucy's doubts and unhappiness were the result of non-communication. Ell too had waited months to hear from Lucy, not knowing the reason for her silence.

Upon Ell's recovery in the fall and his conversation with Lucy's friend Emeline, he carefully penned a letter to Lucy, cautiously addressing her:

Dear Friend
If I may Still call you So, I think I must inform you that I have not received eny reply to a cirtain Lettor I wrote you on the 28th of July and mailed at Port Henry Just three Days Before I was taken Sick. From that time to this I have not herde one word from you, But I will not Chide you to much this time for if I do you may not answer this

It is tru that I was Some Put out By youre not writing to me untill I saw Emeline I then Began to think you had not received my lettor She tolde me the conversation She had with you in regard to a cirtain young Lady who tuck Care of me while I was Sick.

But Beleive it not it is an idle tale For I am still yours and yours only I have not changed let others talk as much as they will I care not my Love is all yours I have non for eny other, I Should not Bee a man if I did not feal gratefull to those two young Ladies for the care they tuck of me while I was sick at Whitehall, had it not Been for them thare would Bee Some Douts a Bout my Beeing here at the Present time.

And had they been of the lowist Class of Sirvent Girls and Dun me the Same Kindeness my Fealings would Bee the Same   I Should have felt the Gratitude that I feal now, But Anuf of this   I hope you place a nuf confidance in me as to let Such Idle tales have But little wait with you and Beleive me when I Say that I feal the Saim Fond regard for you that I did when we last Sat in youre Mothers Parlor Side By Side, I am as truly yours now as then, and unless you change, you nead not look for a change in me

I Should have Been at youre house before this time if it had not Been for Sickness. I had while in New York another attack of the Same Kind that I first had Only not So hard and from that time to this I have not Seene a well Day I am now in Champlain with out a living Beaing on Board But my Self So you can sea that I have not had eny chance to leave this Sloop But as Soon as I can I Shall Start for youre place for it Seames a very long time Sence I Saw you last and I can truly Say that it is lonsom a nuf here a lone. I will now Bring my letter to a close for my head aches and I cannot See to write.

> From your Friend and well wisher
>   E B Rockwell

...you may look for me the first hevy rain Storm after this. I Shal Expect a letter Before long. . . . So Good by for the Present

> Truly yours
>   E.B.R.
> Champlain   Oct the 3rd 1855
>   Direct to Alburgh[49]

As he had promised, Ell had shown up at Lucy's door not long after his letter. After such near disastrous misunderstandings, he asked her to marry him without many more months of delay.

As an additional apology, Ell surprised Lucy with a poem. She would cherish and keep it always, along with his letters:

> Truce to thy fond misgivings
> These fruitless tears guive [sic] one
> No absence can divide us love
> No parting part us more
> Mountains and seas may rest between
> To mock our baffled will
> But heart in heart and soul in soul
> We bide together still
> Where ere I go or far or near
> I cannot be alone
> Thy voice is ever in mine ere
> Thy hand pressed in my own.
> Thy head upon my pillow rests
> Thy words my bosom thrill
> And heart in heart and soul in soul
> We bide together still.[50]

Fortunately for Lucy and Ell, they were able to patch up their courtship and finally marry. It was helpful that the two of them were of the same economic background and that their parents were agreeable to their marriage. But that was not always the case. Abraham Lincoln broke an engagement because he himself could see that she "would not be satisfied. There is a great deal of flourishing about in carriages here, which it would be your doom to see without shareing [sic] in it. You would have to be poor without the means of hiding your poverty. Do you believe you could bear that patiently? Whatever woman may cast her lot with mine, should any ever do so, it is my intention to do all in my power to make her happy and contented; and there is nothing I can immagine [sic], that would make me more unhappy than to fail in the effort. I know I should be much happier with you than the way I am, provided I saw no signs of discontent in you. . . . My opinion is that you had better not do it."[51]

Perhaps Lincoln broke his engagement with Mary Todd for eighteen months for the same reason. She was from a wealthy, socially prominent family; Lincoln was only a poor, lanky lawyer from the backwoods. In the end it is said their marriage was "the triumph of romantic love over family opposition and snobbery."[52] Mary must have successfully convinced him that she did not mind watching others "flourishing about in carriages," that she did not mind appearing poor. She would be happy and contented with her beloved Mr. Lincoln.[53]

Victorian courtship also had its set of strict rules to be followed. For Sophia Heller in Milwaukee, making an exception just one time forced her to be engaged immediately. As she explained it, after President Lincoln's assassination in April of 1865, she and her beau, Philip Goldsmith, went to see President Lincoln lying in state at the courthouse. Mr. G., as she always referred to him, "insisted that I take his arm as the crowd was so large, but I was so timid I halfway refused but finally had to consent in order not to be separated. In those days if a girl was seen on the arm of a gentleman she was considered to be an engaged girl and, as usual, his sister-in-law had to see us." Properly, Mr. G. proposed to Sophia, who was only a "little over fifteen years of age."[54]

In spite of strait-laced Victorian rules, a young girl used all kinds of subtle ways to flirt: with her eyes, her mouth, and in gestures with her handkerchief. There were twenty-two different motions she could make with that one small square of linen. She hoped the man also knew the language of the handkerchief, so that he did not miss her saying "I love you" by drawing it across her cheek or, heaven forbid, his embarrassment and dejection if she drew her handkerchief through her hands instead, letting him know she hated him. If she twirled it in her left hand, she was saying, "I wish to be rid of you"; in the right hand, "I love another."[55]

Signing each of the couple's names on an item during courtship was believed to bring bad luck. Andrew Johnson was only sixteen and a poor tailor when he had fallen in love with Sarah Word and begun courting her. During their courtship he helped his sweetheart to make a white-work quilt of cambric with stuffed flowers, grapes, leaves, hearts and cornucopias. In one corner Sarah stitched her initials. Andrew's initials were to be stitched in another corner *after* their marriage. Sadly for the young couple, Sarah's mother would not allow this marriage, seeing that he was "poor, young, and lacked social status appropriate for 'a promising South Carolina beauty.'"[56] Mrs. Word had no idea then that this same young man would one day be sworn into the office of President of the United States.

As in the case of Sarah Word and Andrew Johnson, parental approval could be a problem. Even though in some places the legal marrying age was twelve for girls and fourteen for boys, parents' consent was customary. On the frontier, however, with girls so scarce, a man did not have time to dally. If he waited one week, his sweetheart might be grabbed up by another the next Saturday. In 1850 in California, Bernhard Marks wrote of the difficulty in "securing a <u>grown</u> lady, i.e., from 12 upwards" as a dance partner, let alone a wife and, to make matters even more difficult, if not impossible, a Jewish wife.[57]

Having experienced past "defeats" courting, and fearing that if he allowed days to pass he would lose his girl, the legendary frontiersman Davy Crockett in Tennessee "quit trying" with his sweetheart's Irish mother and took matters into his own hands. "All I cared for," he later wrote, "was, to have her daughter on my side, which I knowed was the case then; but how soon some other fellow might knock my nose out of joint again, I couldn't tell." Feeling "rather insulted at the old lady," Davy was determined not to get married in her house: "And so I told her girl, that I would come the next Thursday, and bring a horse, bridle, and saddle for her, and she must be ready to go. Her mother declared I shouldn't have her; but I know'd I should, if somebody else didn't get her before Thursday." On his way home that day he stopped by the justice of the peace "and made a bargain with him to marry me."[58]

Not all men were in such a hurry to find a wife and marry her. In Rhode Island, William J. Brown, the son of freed slaves, was much more discerning and cautious. He was well-educated and an established shoemaker when he discovered himself stricken by love and needing to settle the question of matrimony. He "enjoyed [himself] much in her society" on formal visits. "It was common for ladies to be prepared for company during the evening; then one could find no fault with their appearance," but he "desired to know something of her personal appearance during the day, when engaged in her domestic affairs." Cleverly he devised a plan where he "would drop something during the evening which would cause [him] to call after during the next day." He would go after those things at all different hours of the day. Fortunately for his intended, he found her "trim, dressed according to her work" and in "every way qualified, so far as domestic affairs were concerned, to make a suitable companion for any one, whether in high or low degree."[59] They were married three months later.

On the eastern seacoast, from New England (except for New Hampshire) through the South, "hasty marriages were not approved of at all." It was the law that the intention of marriage or wedding banns must "be published three weeks or three public days before marriage; or be cried in church

ENGAGEMENT RING

It is bad luck to lose or damage an engagement ring. Never let another girl try on the ring, or the bride's future happiness is jeopardized.

The fiancé's birthstone is lucky for an engagement ring.

The diamond was not popular until the nineteenth century, when the exploitation of South African diamond deposits made it relatively inexpensive.

which was to have the town clerk holler it out as loud as he could as soon as the services were over for three Sundays."[60] And, if the bride and groom were from different places, the banns had to be published in each place.

In 1760, John Adams wrote of an even more complex problem of men with dual residences, such as those employed on Castle Island, the fortified post in Boston harbor. Even though these men lived elsewhere, "The Castle Men are all considered as Inhabitants of Boston, so that No Minister will marry a Castle Man, till a Certificate is produced that he has been published in Boston."[61]

On March 19, 1849, Elizabeth Ann Jennison wrote into her diary only three words, "We were published," but those words meant the beginning of "a new era in my life — and henceforth I shall live in another home — under other circumstances than these. . . . A new life comes to me — bearing all glad brightness on its dawning & giving me hope — while yet anxious thoughts of weakness & insufficiency crowd thick into my mind."[62]

For three consecutive Sundays in February of 1852, at the Spring Hill Baptist Church in Mansfield, Connecticut, a loud male voice had called out, "Mr Ephraim Howard of Eastford, and Miss Lucinda L. Place of Mansfield, Intend Marriage." A simple strip of lined paper with the same statement in beautiful script was also tacked up on the door. On the third and final Sunday that their banns were publicly read and posted, the minister wrote onto the back of the paper, "The within was made public on the Sabbath by me. A.S. Atwood. Mansfield Feb. 22. 1852."[63] It was finally legal for the couple to marry, and they *were* married, that very day.

Banns of marriage of Lucinda Place and Ephraim Howard, Mansfield, Connecticut, 1852. *Courtesy of Ethel Golden Nichols, granddaughter of the couple.*

Front

Back

Even in the Ohio territory "it was necessary that notice should be given, either in writing posted at some conspicuous place within the township where the woman resided, or publicly declared on two days of public worship." But in such rough country "sometimes a notice written on a piece of paper, and signed 'D.C. Cooper, Justice of the Peace,' was tacked to the trunk of a large forest tree close to a road."[64]

Quakers also could not marry quickly. The Quaker woman must pass "the first meeting," in which she proposed taking another Quaker in marriage, and "hereby offered her decision for the approbation of Friends." Later the bride-elect had to pass another meeting, "declaring that her intention still continued the same, and then, no objection being offered, the arrangements for the marriage were concluded."[65]

Of course, in spite of laws, there were those young couples that ran away to elope. For some young women, far from the protection of family and friends, the results were disastrous. An extreme case was of "a young person [who] came to a house in that city [Boston] for board, who, it was discovered, was in reality a young woman dressed in male apparel. Upon being questioned she at once acknowledged that it was so. She stated that she had lately been at work at a mill in Manchester, N.H.; that she had agreed to elope with a young man who had promised to marry her, and had assumed the disguise to prevent trouble. Upon her arrival here the man deserted her and she was at a perfect loss what to do with herself. She was given up to Mr. John Augustus, who at once had her clothed in female apparel. Her hair had been cut short, but a straggling long hair or two had been left and first excited the suspicion of the people of the house as to her sex. She stated that she had a father and mother living in Vermont."[66]

Until the end of the eighteenth century, it was not uncommon for girls to be married at very young ages in the eastern states. Grandmother Cutler, a Virginian belle and niece of General Francis Marion, "was married at fourteen to Colonel Herne and the tradition of her grief at parting with her dolls on her wedding morning still survives."[67] Generally over the years, however, in the more civilized parts of the country, women began marrying at much older ages. By 1800 in New England, 19 to 23 was her average age; by 1830 she was as old as 23 to 26. In the South in the early 1800's, girls were still marrying at young ages. An English comedian around 1800 was surprised that the Virginia ladies married nearly ten years earlier than those in Europe and that by twenty "if she had proved a fruitful olive, her husband's table was surrounded with tall shoots sufficient to supply him with shade for the remainder of his days." And it was reported that in North Carolina the girls were married so young that many were grandmothers by the time they reached twenty-seven years of age.[68]

On the frontier in new territories of the west, necessity ruled. In the Ohio territory in 1800, laws for marrying were "of male persons of the age of eighteen and female persons of the age of fourteen, and not nearer of kin than first cousins. . . . Early marriages were so much the custom that respectable parents saw with approbation young daughters who at the present day [1896]

MONTHS FOR MARRIAGE

Marry in September's shine,
Your living will be rich and fine.
If in October you do marry,
Love will come but riches tarry.
If you wed in bleak November,
Only joy will come, remember.
When December's showers fall fast,
Marry and true love will last.

Marry in May
Rue for aye.
   May marriages were avoided. Death or
misfortune was sure to follow. A child born
of a May marriage is sickly.

Married in Lent
You'll live to repent

June was considered a lucky month by the
Romans, especially at times of the full or new
moon. June was supposedly derived from and
sacred to Juno.

would still be in the school-room married to men who were mere boys in age. A girl of fifteen was as much a young lady in 1800 as a girl of twenty at the present day."[69] In Kentucky, "a marriage that sometimes united a boy of sixteen to a girl of fourteen was an occasion of merriment and brought out the whole fort."[70] Especially in the early years in Texas, brides were very young, some only fourteen or fifteen years of age. A young man attended a wedding: the bride "was not quite sixteen. Just a good age," he noted.[71]

In the mid-nineteenth century, the federal land law in Oregon *forced* men to find a wife: as single men, they could obtain only a half section; married, an entire section of land. Consequently, mail-order brides were common, as well as brides of very young age. Supposedly "it was not uncommon to see brides of fourteen." Some of those married women were seen "in the woods of the Columbia playing with their dolls."[72]

There was much controversy in the East concerning mail-order brides.

LEFT: Oriyo Shiote in Japan prior to her departure for America. *Photograph courtesy of Yoshiye Sato Tsuboi.*
Oriyo was nineteen or younger at the time of this photograph. This may have been the photograph sent to Shiroye Sato in Oregon, making her a "picture bride." Later, in Oregon, Oriyo cut up her native silk kimonos and made futons out of them.

RIGHT: Shiroye and Oriyo Shiote Sato in their wedding suits. *Photograph courtesy of Yoshiye Sato Tsuboi.*
Unlike in Japan, in Oregon Oriyo had to be very frugal. She wore her wedding suit for many years, then only the jacket for years longer. Her oldest daughter, Masaye, remembers wearing "the jacket part of it to grade school. It was sort of a khaki type — tannish color, a wool, sort of a hard, tightly woven material. It wore well." Masaye's younger sister added that Oriyo "finally just threw it away — she had to wear it so much."

The *New York World* wrote, "Boston girls do not take kindly to the proposition to reduce the surplus of marriageable young women in that city by deporting them in 'job lots' to the new states of the far West to meet the demand there for wives.

"One of the bright and pretty sales girls interviewed on the subject by a *World* reporter said: 'When I get married it will be after one of the old-fashioned courtships.' She scouted the idea of jumping into a matrimonial grab-bag to get a husband, and declined as wholly unsatisfactory the plan of a courtship by correspondence."[73]

For Oriyo Shiote Sato, a photo bride leaving Hiroshima, Japan, by ship headed for America, there had been neither courtship nor love. Her marriage had been prearranged between families in Japan, her future husband in Oregon having seen only her photograph.

Nineteen-year-old Oriyo "didn't look like the usual country girl."[74] Under five feet tall and very pretty, she was a well-educated young lady from a merchant's family. Although her attributes had quickly won her a husband, they would be of little value upon her arrival in frontier America.

For the rest of her life, Oriyo wished only to forget her first experiences. The journey had been terrible; many seasick, frightened young women like herself all crowded together on a miserable ship. Then, when she had finally arrived at immigration in Tacoma, Washington, she was kept back because of her eyesight and "didn't get to join her friends."[75] For the first time she had been all by herself in a strange country, unable to speak the language or communicate with anyone.

But that had been only the prelude to the hard life and terrible hardships she would have to endure. Quickly, she had been married and taken to her husband's land above the saw mill in Dee, Oregon. As a new bride, she had no choice but to work alongside this stranger, her husband, clearing his forested land until "her hands wouldn't even close at night."[76] Then, to earn cash, they journeyed by train, steamer, and crude wagons to pick hopsacks for days on end. For newly married Shiroye and Oriyo, there was only constant, grueling, back-breaking work: "they didn't know what love was."[77] Always, Oriyo yearned to go back to Japan, to return to the good, refined life she had once taken for granted.

In all parts of the country, great age differences between men and women were not uncommon. Women died young in childbearing or from disease. They were especially prone to consumption because of exhaustion and poor diets in new settlements. A widower re-married quickly, most often needing a mother for his cabin full of tiny, helpless children. Men looked to their deceased wives' younger sisters, cousins and unmarried neighbor women. Because available women were scarce, especially in new settlements, it was not uncommon for a man to marry two or three sisters in his lifetime; when one would die, the next girl in line would have reached her teens, and she would mother her older sister's (or sisters') babies.

In the Savannah *Ladies' Magazine* of 1819 were reports of several unusual circumstances. In one, a man seventy-five married a girl of twelve who was the daughter of his former wife, and his new bride's brother married the

HISTORY OF THE WEDDING RING

The oldest rings are found in Egypt. "Before the introduction of coinage, Egyptian gold was circulated in the form of rings. The husband placed one of them on his wife's finger to show that he entrusted her with his property." Ethel L. Urlin, A Short History of Marriage (Detroit: Singing Tree Press, 1969), p. 227.

The wedding ring was worn by the ancient Romans and sometimes among the Jews; from these it became a part of the Christian marriage.

The Anglo-Saxons' keys to all their worldly goods were hung on a ring which was worn on the married woman's finger.

The Puritans objected to the wedding ring in the ceremony, so the wife put it on quietly afterwards.

Betrothal rings were in shapes symbolic of love. An amphisbaena, or serpent with its tail in its mouth, meant eternal love; a pair of clasped hands is one of the oldest symbols of plighted troth. In the fourteenth and fifteenth centuries they were inscribed in "posies" (poesies) or verses: "This and my heart," "Not two but one till life be gone." In the nineteenth century, wedding rings were also commonly engraved. Abraham Lincoln had Mary Todd's engraved, "Love is Eternal." In minuscule lettering legible only with a jeweler's glass, Morris Golden inscribed his beloved Mary Howard's ring, "Each for the other, both for God MWG to MEH October 21, 1890."

groom's daughter.[78]

There was another age-old reason why men chose to marry women years younger than themselves. In *Godey's Magazine and Lady's Book* of 1844, an "ancient lady" was turned down and insulted because of her age when she went after her choice during leap year. She told him "that a person of his age ought to select a woman of maturity for a wife, not a chit in her teens, unable to appreciate the value of the sacrifice he made." To that he said, "You are too old to become my wife." She "shrieked" that he was "ancient enough" to be her father. Insulting her further, Mr. Cremone said, "A man is in his prime at fifty — a woman at five and twenty, or, at the most, thirty; consequently I have barely climbed to the top of the hill, while you have passed over it, and are very considerably down the wrong side. I have seen many a young couple, of equal ages, boy and girl, 'made for each other,' as the wiseacres say, pair off in the spring of life.... In twelve years or so, the boy has become a man, but the girl is an old woman."[79]

The extremes in ages were not always good; in many instances they were disastrous, especially in promoting wife (or, in many instances, actually child) abuse. Elvina Apperson Fellows was one of nine children. Her father had "died on the way across the plains," and her "mother had no money and had nine hungry mouths to fill in addition to her own." As Elvina later said, "In 1851 Mother was pretty hard run to earn enough money for us to live on, so when a man named Julius Thomas, a cook in a restaurant, offered to marry me, Mother thought I had better take him, so I did. He was 44 and I was 14. Back in 1851 ... we had slavery of Negroes in the South, and we had slavery of wives all over the United States, and saloons wherever there were enough people to make running one pay. What could a girl of 14 do to protect herself from a man of 44, particularly if he drank most of the time, as my husband did? When he was drunk he often wanted to kill me, and he used to beat me until I thought I couldn't stand it." Finally Elvina had escaped to her mother's house and locked the door. He had tried to climb into the window, but she "held it down." Then he became so enraged that he "took out his pistol and shot" at her. It scared Elvina so much that she dropped to the floor. Believing he had killed her, he "put the end of the pistol barrel into his mouth and pulled the trigger."[80] Thankfully, Elvina was a widow.

For Mary Allen, the story had a very tragic ending. "Born out of wedlock," at 13 she was married to a thirty-five-year-old, Adam Wimple. That very first year he killed her and set fire to the house so that no one would know. Unfortunately for Mr. Wimple, neighbors rushed to the fire and put it out, discovering that Mary had been murdered. In October of 1852 he was hanged in Dallas.[81]

Matilda Jane Sager Delaney also was married at a young age to a much older man. In her case, however, she married to escape the "terror and bitterness" of her childhood. Enroute to Oregon, both of her parents had died of mountain fever, leaving Matilda, age four, and her six brothers and sisters orphans. Matilda was severely abused by her various guardians, "welts or black and blue marks" all over her body from "constant beatings." In her teens she was whipped so much that the neighbors complained, but the judge sympathized with her guardian. Understandably Matilda married a thirty-one-year-old miner named I. M. Hazlett, instead of being forced back into her intolerable situation. She had been fifteen then, and she had gone to the gold mines of California with her husband. Eight years later he died. Matilda, only twenty-three and with five children, took in washing to support herself and the children.[82]

In villages and towns young women opened the newspaper to read the tiny column "Marriages." They looked forward to the festivities of a friend's or family member's wedding. As they scoured the yellow pine floor with chapped, reddened hands, or swished pantaloons and shirts up and down in boiling lye water, wives remembered the day when they had promised "to love and to cherish till death. . . ."

As the country was in varying degrees of settlement, so were the kinds of weddings. No matter how poor or simple, however, there was almost always some kind of festivities, usually the best the family could afford. Most weddings were at the bride's home. For many, home was a tiny log cabin in a clearing in the woods. Others might have been fortunate enough to have moved out of that first cramped, one-room log house and into a larger, two-story house on their land, such as the farmer "far up in the wilds of New Hampshire . . . a new settler, who had just cleared his farm and erected his buildings." That farmer admitted that he "was in but a poor fix to accommodate wedding guests"; nevertheless, there was a "bridal pair" waiting to be married. His newly finished house was unfurnished, but they had made do the best they could:

On the table, set into the middle of the room, were burning two large tallow candles, each fixed into a huge potato, shaved and drilled to the purpose. On the wall, directly in front of where it was intended the bridal pair should stand, four other candles were fastened by steel tined forks; one of which, stooping a little from its perpendicular, was sending long channels of tallow down to the floor. The guests were seated on wooden benches around the room, still and fixed as a row of pins in paper; and, as the light from time to time required snuffing, some lusty fellow would rise, and, wetting his fingers from his mouth before each operation, would render the service, in a measure, that, I am sure, the unpractised could never imitate.[83]

The bride too had made do with what she had at the moment. She "was arrayed in a sarsanet cambric morning robe . . . , tied up and down in front, over a petticoat of bright red flannel, with blue worsted hose, and cowhide shoes peeping from below; a string of gold beads surrounding the neck, and a dark horn comb ambitiously aspiring above the croppled-crowned head of whitest hair."[83]

Her dress, although announcing her extremely poor circumstances, was the best that she had at the time. For the country girl across America, this was not only fashionably acceptable in the community, but she herself expected nothing more. From the deep-seated roots of her religious upbringing, she had learned the importance of practicality and frugality, of simplicity and

DAYS FOR MARRIAGE

Monday for wealth,
Tuesday for health,
Wednesday best day of all,
Thursday for losses,
Friday for crosses,
And Saturday, no luck at all.

In New England, no one married on Friday: it was hangman's day.

Early on, Sunday was a good day for marriage. In the nineteenth century, however, it was a complete day of rest, a day for renewing oneself, not a good day for a wedding.

44

humility rather than vanity and pride. Her dress reflected this. Although it was the best dress she could afford, it was also a dress she could wear later for meetings and other weddings for years to come. Surprisingly, many country brides of the late eighteenth and first quarter of the nineteenth century wore white — linen homespun, many times of their own making or, if they were able to purchase cloth, a very sheer cotton mull, cambric or dimity.

At that period white was a fashionable best dress for all young women, just as the white day dress became fashionable in the early twentieth century. In 1802, when Samuel Paine was making sugar, "12 girls [came] horse back, all dressed in white. I had them all to wait on and to hitch their horses." He added to his autobiography, "They were very lively and had a nice time, and they made hills of sugar and carried a lot of it home in that shape."[84] Since white was a young woman's best dress, it was practical that she also wear it for her wedding.

For a widow, no matter her circumstances or age, the traditional white was forbidden. For many years the white wedding bonnet was the most important item of attire denoting a first marriage. One young woman, married and widowed all at the age of seventeen, was "exceedingly unhappy because, having been a widow, she could not in etiquette appear in a white bonnet and feathers and veil." Instead she wore a bonnet of "shirred gray velvet with natural gray feathers and cherry-colored face trimmings of very full ruches of ribbon loops" for her "coming out bride" after her second marriage. She felt "so conspicuous" not being able to wear white, just "like an old woman."[85] Surprisingly, the German bride in Pennsylvania in the eighteenth century would have felt the same embarrassment if she were not married in a black silk hood.

When Dolly Payne married John Todd, she could not wear a white wedding dress or "veil of lace or tulle." She was a Quaker and had to dress in appropriate drab style.

> Her wedding gown was ashen silk,
> Too simple for her taste.
> She wanted lace about the neck
> And a ribbon at the waist.[86]

In fact, twenty-one-year-old Dolly, "so fond of everything gay and brilliant," had to "forego the dancing and wine-drinking, the stealing of slippers, and mischievous merry-making which marked wedding festivities among the world's people, for the decorum and solemnity of the Quaker marriage."[86]

But it was not the woman who was denied a white wedding bonnet or bridal dress who should be pitied. Truly the woman to be pitied was she who had no choice but a "shift," "smock," or "closet" marriage, for she had to be married barefoot with only a loose shift or no clothes or accessories on her person whatsoever. According to a nineteenth-century explanation, "It was an opinion prevalent in those days [through the first quarter of the nineteenth century] that whoever married a widow who was administratrix upon the estate of her deceased husband, and who through her came into possession of anything purchased by the first husband, became liable for any demands against the first husband's estate."[87]

This difficulty could be avoided if the widow were married completely naked. After all, according to the law, everything she had was the property of her husband, even the linens and bedding of her own spinning and weaving that she had brought with her in her wedding outfit, even her own babies, *literally everything* belonged solely to her husband.

At first these marriages were called "smock-marriages" or "shift marriages," and "usually for modesty's sake, this ceremony took place in the evening."[88] A man and woman met to be married on the King's Highway, the bride being allowed by the law to wear only a shift, absolutely nothing else. One such wedding was recorded by Jeremiah Angell, Justice of the Peace in Rhode Island: "I hereby certify that Isaac Howard of Scituate in the County of Providence &c. Took Hepsozed Darbee a poor Widow Woman as She

COLORS

The traditional color of the Virgin's robe, blue represents constancy. The custom of wearing "something blue" is said to be from the ancient Israelites, the bride wearing a "ribband of blue" over her shoulder meaning "purity, love and fidelity." William J. Fielding, Strange Customs of Courtship and Marriage *(New York: The New Home Library, 1942), p. 47.*

Yellow is the classic color of Hymen, the god of marriage. As it is also the color of the flame, in Roman times the flame-yellow veil was the most important part of the bride's attire. Saffron-colored shoes were also important. In eighteenth-century America yellow, usually in heavy brocades, was the favorite color for the bride. Blue was second in popularity, lilac third. Red, the color of defiance, was worn by many brides during the Revolutionary War.

Gold was a proper color to wear for a second marriage in the seventeenth century.

White and silver gowns were in vogue in the eighteenth century. By 1750 many British brides were wearing white satin and lace.

come to him in the Kings Highway in her sheft in sd Scituate aforesd to be his Wife and that they the sd Isaac and the sd Hepsozed was Lawfully joined Together in marriage the 7th day of April 1770 in the aforesd Highway in the presence of Capt Thomas Fry, Benajah Place and Benjamin Wells and others before me the Subscriber."[89]

Could Hepsozed have loved this man so much that she was willing to appear in a poor, loose-fitting piece of homespun to be married with the eyes of curious men watching on? Or was the truth that he would have her no other way? Regardless, it is doubtful that she would ever forget her humiliation and shame, as well as her overwhelming disappointment, at not being married in her best dress. The widow Mary Bradley, "clad only in her shift,"[90] was so cold and shaking on a bitter February day that the minister threw his coat over her.

It was only later that a bride was able to "take her stand in a closet,"[91] instead of on the King's Highway. But in "closet marriages" she was not permitted to wear even a shift. There were many different ways devised for this type of wedding. When Mr. Averill was married to his second wife, "A blanket was stretched across a recess next the chimney, behind which went the bride with her attendants, who divested her of all her clothing, and threw her clothes into the room. She then reached her hand through a small opening in the blanket, which was clasped by Mr. Averill, and the marriage ceremony was performed. He then produced a complete assortment of wedding attire which was appropriated by Mrs. Averill, who soon appeared in full dress, to receive the congratulations of her friends."[92]

In another closet marriage, the bride "stood, with no clothing on, within a closet and held out her hand to the major through a diamond-shaped hole in the door. When the two had been pronounced man and wife, she came forth from the closet, gorgeously attired in wedding garments, which had been thoughtfully placed there for her use."[93]

Without any sympathy for the embarrassed bride, such weddings were indiscreetly published in the town newspaper. One such marriage notice appeared in the *Salem Gazette* of April 21, 1818: "At St. Johns, Mr. Samuel — to Mrs. —, widow. She was in a state of nudity while the ceremony was performed, which according to an old custom exonerates the new husband from any liability for the former husband's debts."[94]

Traditionally it was unlucky to make your own wedding gown, but for many brides that was necessary. Many made their own; they had to. Anna Spaulding was nineteen when she married Samuel Laughton in December of 1786 in a "linen muslin dress of her own manufacture. She selected the nicest flax, hatcheled, carded and spun the same into a thread so fine that each skein consisting of fourteen knots, could be drawn through her open thimble. The dress was woven, cut and made by herself, and in texture resembled silk."[95]

In Dedham, Massachusetts, four years later, Priscilla Guild's family was able to purchase the white cloth and satin for her wedding. In spite of its being a very cold day in February, she wore "a short white dress over a beautiful white satin skirt, cut in gores ... high-heeled shoes with silver

COLORS

Married in white,
You have chosen all right.
Married in gray,
You will go far away.
Married in black,
You will wish yourself back.
Married in red,
You'd better be dead.
Married in green,
Ashamed to be seen.
Married in blue,
You'll always be true.
Married in pearl,
You'll live in a whirl.
Married in yellow,
Ashamed of the fellow.
Married in brown,
You'll live out of town.
Married in pink,
Your spirit will sink.

Contributed by Augusta W. Thompson, Springfield, Vermont. Vermont Quarterly, XXIII (1955), 264.

HENRY E. PEACH

Detail of the hem of the white muslin wedding dress worn by Marion Chandler for her wedding to Dr. Hiram Holt at Pomfret,
Connecticut, on February 21, 1828. *Collection of Old Sturbridge Village, Sturbridge, Massachusetts.*
Marion was 27 years old. According to a note attached to the dress, she stitched all the elaborate white work: the exquisite scalloped
border, net inlay, cutwork, french knots and satin-stitched flowers.

buckles, and her hair was combed, brushed and powdered . . . her linen handkerchief was spun by herself. . . . A bridesmaid and a bridesman held two burning candles over their heads as the minister pronounced them man and wife."[96] Her father gave her a dowry including a cow.

Indeed there was nothing so unusual about a white wedding gown. White was a simple gown for the country girl to make — after all, it could be completely of her family's own manufacture, from planting and growing the flax to spinning, weaving, cutting and sewing. Everything about her gown could be the product of her home. She had the same opportunity to have an exquisite white gown as any other young woman in the countryside. But at that point, ability, perfection and skill made the difference. The flax hatcheled over and over, the finest linen thread spun, the most skilled weaver — these made the difference in the bride's wedding gown before factory cloth was available and affordable.

Also married in white, Bessie, a poor minister's daughter, believed

with her limited means it would be far better to be married in an ordinary dress, than to spend the money she so much needed for furnishing her house, in purchasing one for a ceremony that, in the performance, would not occupy at the longest more than ten minutes of time, with none to witness it but her own family.... The dress she had worn that day to meeting, and in which she proposed to be married, was a pelisse flannel of a crimson hue. Being told by a friend, that to wear red upon such an occasion was a sign she would quarrel with her husband, although not a believer in signs, she changed her mind, and concluded to be married in white. She ran to her room in haste, for she had but a few moments in which to select and arrange her dress; there was no time lost in deciding, for she had but one white dress. It had not been worn during the winter, and it happened to be clean. The material was dimity; the skirt contained but three breadths, was cut goring, and upon the bottom was a flounce of cambric, an eighth of a yard in depth.[97]

As the frontier pushed westward, so did the spinning wheels and looms. When John and Mary Crownover Rabb were moving from one homesite to another in Spanish Texas, they loaded all their household possessions onto a horse and oxen. "On the packhorse Flacus the clothes were placed first; then the iron kettle. Next the skillet and lid were piled, and last the spinning wheel, which rose along the top." When one of the pigs "wandered under a cow's hoof and was lamed," it was fastened on the packhorse *under* the spinning wheel. But the "pig's squealing and squirming caused Flacus to bolt, scattering his pack on the ground and killing the pig, and Mary bemoaned the loss of her cooking pot, which was 'broke all to bits.'" Amazingly, the cumbersome spinning wheel made the long trip undamaged, and Mary resumed her spinning inside their tent. Mary was sheltered as she spun, but only the head of her spinning wheel fit under their crude tent made out of a quilt and a homespun sheet. The rest of her wheel had to withstand the inhospitable wind, dirt and rain of the Texas prairie. Later the Rabbs moved north to a rough camp. There Mary continued to spin "enough thread for forty-six yards of 'muscato baring.'" And she had her husband "build her a loom, then a twenty-foot-square house, and a shed for her loom."[98]

No matter how small the pioneer's first log, sod or dugout home, these proportionately large, unwieldy items maintained their place by the hearth — even though generations on the other side of the Appalachians were turning to the modern conveniences. By the second quarter of the nineteenth century, textile mills were looming over many New England villages. Men could purchase cloth now for their wives and daughters. The older women continued to spin, but as soon as American factory-made cloth was available and inexpensive, the young women prepared for their wedding outfits simply by seaming and hand-hemming yardage, their girlhood skills of spinning and weaving no longer necessary; in fact, those skills were quickly becoming obsolete.

By the time Lucinda Place was making her wedding outfit in Mansfield, Connecticut, she could buy American, factory-made lengths of bleached

A piece of the wedding dress of
Eunice Brigham who married
Elijah Royce Feb 23rd 1788

A piece of the wedding dress of
Laura Royce who married
Jason Kendall Sept 16th 1817

A piece of the wedding dress of
Mrs Betsey Royce Brigham who married
Elisha Morey Feb 21st 1841

A piece of the wedding dress of
Mary Chase who married
Carlos N Brigham

A piece of the wedding dress and trimming
of Laura H Brigham who married
Edwin C Hoadley Jan 1st 1852

A piece of the wedding dress of
Augusta Havens who married
Charles F Brigham

A piece of the wedding dress of
Maria E Hoadley who married
Benj F Larned Oct 21. 1856.

Julia A Lincoln married
Jason Kendall Hoadley
Jan 14th 1871

wedding dress of
Laura Kendall who married Maddison Slayton

A piece of the wedding dress of
Marilla C Slayton who married
Stephen Kittridge

A piece of the wedding dress of
Ella Blake who married Charlie Washburn

A piece of the wedding dress and cloak
of Lucy Ann Holt who married
Daniel Perry of Stoneham Mass

A piece of the wedding dress of
Mary Burnham who married
Lucian Morgan

A piece of the wedding dress of
Hattie Cabot who married Horace Dennis

A piece of the wedding dress of
Abba M Slayton who married
Harvey Thomas

A piece of the wedding dress of
Lizie French who married
Joseph Makenzie of Adrian
Mich

A piece of the wedding dress
of Mary Ann French who married
Larnard C Kendall Jan 1st 1851

Hartland. 1889.

Maranda A Roods wedding dress
married to Joseph S Holt
Jan 15th 1837

L. M. Burlington
Lizzie M Brewster
Married
June 30th 1859

E. M. Goodwin
Fellen A Brewster
married March 17. 1859

Wedding dres: of Mrs Sally C
married. Isaac Hartwell

Herman Wollace Hoadley
Elmina Buckman Howe
married April 15 186

George Abbat Hitt
Edith Maria Hoadly
married March 188

May W Larned married
Oliver P Kibben
June 1893

...nice Parker Wiley
married
John Knights
April 1893

Mary Townsend
married
Bert Bowen

Maria Boynton
married
Oliva Smith

Eliza Burnham
married
John M. Blake

Clara Atwood
and
Mr Stewart
married June 1903

...urtra L ...cal...
married
Henry W Walker

Mrs Estabrook
married
Mr Byron Thomas
June 3rd 1900

cotton cloth for her sheets and pillowcases, as well as wonderful, bright calicoes for dresses and quilts. Like her mother before her, "she wanted to have some things for going to housekeeping,"[99] including her two friendship quilts, at least six pairs of cotton sheets and the pillowcases to go with them that she had seamed and hemmed by hand, then marked in little tiny cross-stitch "LLP" with numbers for the inventory and laundering of her linens.

The minister's daughter Bessie also "occupied her evenings in working a white cotton bed-spread. It was worked with cotton roping in flowers of her mother's drawing. In the centre of the spread, was a basket, from which pinks and roses were shooting forth in every direction, with more regularity even, than nature ever produced. Upon the border was a vine filled with clusters of grapes. It was an elaborate design, and very handsome, but would require both time and patience to execute.

"It was the custom, in olden time, to put an immense amount of labor upon bed-quilts. In her girlhood days, Bessie's mother had made for herself two such quilts, that now adorned the parsonage. These were of worsted stuff, one blue and the other scarlet; both quilted in flowers, and stuffed with wool of her own batting, and so thick and closely quilted they would almost stand alone. The scarlet one was used exclusively for the spare bed, giving it always a very gay appearance. Having been accustomed to such herculean tasks herself, accounts for her drawing a pattern so elaborate for Bessie."[100]

In the second quarter of the nineteenth century, there was a new trend for the wedding dress of the countryside — printed cottons and soft, lightweight wools and wool/silk combinations. The gowns were still of the brides' making or that of their mother and sisters, but now the bride of the country wore florals and floral stripes of the best cloth she could afford. This dress would serve as her best dress for as long as she could get into it. And if she were leaving for her new home somewhere a long journey over the mountains, this dress would serve as her journeying dress, or be packed inside the one special trunk reserved for best things, the only extra space she was allowed amidst all the necessities. Upon arriving at her drafty log shanty in new government land or flea-infested dugout on the prairie, she would entertain her lady callers with tea and biscuits in the dress in which she was married. Again practicality was of the upmost importance to the country bride. Her wedding had been but moments in the already distant past; her dress was lasting, and in many cases her most valued piece of clothing. No matter how poor she was in the west, with it she could attend meetings, christenings, weddings and dances dressed perhaps even more elegantly than the nearest, though distant, neighbor woman too many years removed from those fine eastern dresses she had brought with her.

For Flora Whitman Abbott of Abbotts Corner, Quebec, life in the brand-new railroad town of Goff, Kansas, in 1880 was not as she had anticipated. It was very poor there in those years, "clothing and shoes...at a premium." Flora had arrived in this "hilly, hidden, hungry little burg, a young married woman, with a trunk load of lovely clothes." But "when she went to church she found the other folks arrayed in calico gowns, many without hats or even

WEDDING VEIL

Wedding dress, c. 1840, St. Albans, Vermont, hand-sewn of imported printed cottons. *Collection of the author.*

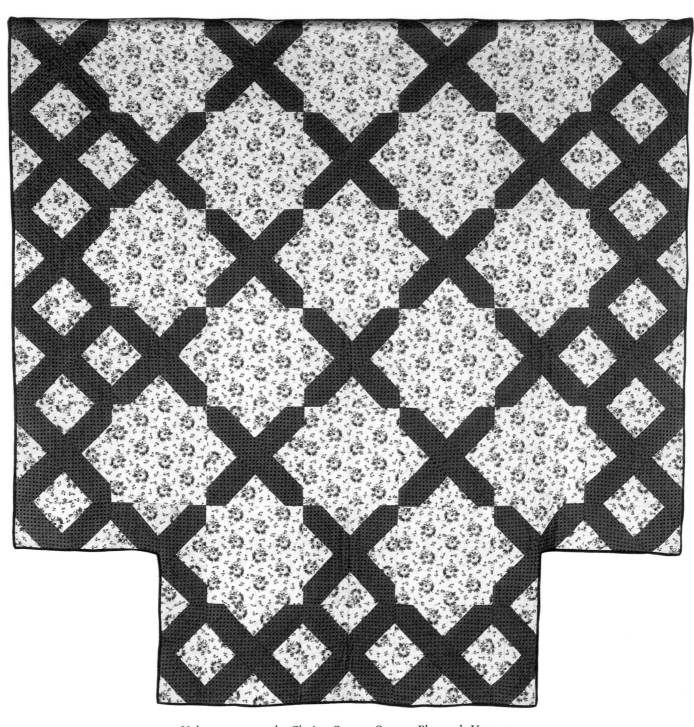

Unknown pattern, by Clarissa Sumner Sawyer, Plymouth, Vermont, c. 1840, 87 × 87 inches, pieced cottons. *Courtesy of Barbara Chiolino and Elizabeth Bailey.*
Clarissa wore a dress of the imported floral print with off-white background for her marriage to Calvin Coolidge Sawyer on November 11, 1838, in Plymouth, Vermont. Both Clarissa and Calvin were blood ancestors of President Calvin Coolidge.

sunbonnets and some without shoes. So she folded away her lovely clothes, got out the plainest things she had, made her others of greater simplicity and went to church and did about as her less fortunate neighbors."[101]

After her marriage, Clarissa Sumner Sawyer went to housekeeping in a tiny log cabin in Vermont. Perhaps it was a difficult moment at the first rip of the seam of her dress and the destructive cut of scissors, but Clarissa was actually preserving the memories of her wedding and dress as she cut up the pretty imported floral cotton and pieced her own pattern into a quilt top.[102]

*T*hen came the wedding of the century, the storybook wedding to change all weddings and to set the fashion for all brides of the future: twenty-year-old Queen Victoria married her beloved cousin Prince Albert, just "after mid-day on Monday 10 February 1840." Traditionally, queens wore "rich brocades...with heavy state robes of velvet and ermine" for their weddings, but Victoria "thought [it] could not be necessary. Much better white,"[103] she wrote into her diary on December 19, 1839. Exciting news of the wedding and her special white bridal gown spread to America. Thousands and thousands of newspapers and periodicals were shared, reaching women in remote new settlements hungering for fineries and romance. Queen Victoria's wedding was the talk.

In the queen's own words, she wore "a white satin gown with a very deep flounce of Honiton lace, imitation of old ... my Turkish diamond necklace and earrings, and Albert's beautiful sapphire brooch." Her hair was dressed and she had a wreath of orange blossoms in it. Two hundred persons had worked constantly from March to November to make the exquisite, one-of-a-kind lace, the flounce of her gown four yards long and three quarters of a yard in depth. Instead of the usual robes of state, Queen Victoria wore a "court train attached to the waist, of white satin trimmed with orange blossom sprays round the edges."[104] Her twelve trainbearers were also dressed in white, of the same material as her own gown.

Immediately her wedding was the "proper style." Soon in America, women could read books, such as the *Art of Good Behavior,* of the proper wedding:

The bride is usually dressed in pure white — she wears a white veil, and her head is crowned with a wreath of white flowers, usually artificial; and orange blossoms are preferred. She should wear no ornaments but such as her intended husband or her father may present her for the occasion — certainly no gift, if any such were retained, of any former sweetheart.

The bridesmaid, or bridesmaids, if there be two, are generally younger than the bride, and should also be dressed in white, but more simply.[105]

Eighteen-year-old Lucy Ann McElroy had followed the style precisely for her wedding to Ell B. Rockwell in Sandy Hill, New York, on January 22, 1856. Her ivory satin wedding gown, with hundreds of pearls of the sea handsewn in the outline of leaves on the bodice and down the front of the skirt, ended in a short train. Wax orange blossoms crowned her long veil of

POPULAR NINETEENTH-CENTURY BRIDAL FLOWERS

Orange blossoms
Symbol of fertility, the orange tree being one of the most fruitful; if artificial they should be removed before the end of the first month of marriage.

Roses
Flowers of Venus, white roses represented virginity; red roses meant love, joy and beauty.

Myrtle
Symbol of constancy in duty and affection; in Wales it was planted on both sides of the front door to bring harmony to the household.

Rosemary
Symbol of remembrance

Baby's breath
Symbol of fertility

Wedding gown, worn by Lucy Ann McElroy at her marriage to steamer pilot Ell B. Rockwell on January 22, 1856, in Sandy Hill, New York, hand-sewn of ivory satin, with pearls. *Collection of the author.*
The hundreds of pearls, hand-sewn down the bodice and skirt, possibly were sent to Lucy by her brother Barney, who was a whaler.

Lucy Ann McElroy's wedding veil with wax orange blossoms, 1856. *Collection of the author.*

silk netting that would hide the mixed emotions in her eyes as Reverend Hitchcock pronounced the young couple man and wife.

The fashion of wedding white early on also reached all parts of rural America. In Athens, Ohio, in October of 1845, at their double wedding, brides Maria Foster and her sister both wore white dresses "made with tucks and lace. That fine, soft, switchy stuff . . . India mull! The skirts were plenty full. . . . We wore white kid shoes and we had orange blossoms in our hair."[106]

White bridal gowns, veils and orange blossoms were the style. Style or not, however, white was extremely impractical in the mid-nineteenth century. At a time when many brides were moving west with their beloveds, white was not only impractical but silly. There was nothing to do with the dress after the wedding. So in spite of the fashion most young women of rural areas continued to wear their best dresses, but now they were of rich, more deeply colored, rustling silks, in many different patterns: figured, striped, plaid.

Then there was conflict on the subject of a white wedding gown for the sophisticated, fashionable young lady who journeyed thousands of miles by ship, stage, train and canal boat to be married in the west. Her reality of a lavish white wedding gown and a church wedding in the east did not make the transition to the rough, new settlements of the west. Mehitable Berry Felton was only fourteen in 1851 when her intended had left Massachusetts headed for California and "inexhaustible" gold.[107] Thirteen years had passed and, in the summer of 1864, Mehitable finally began assembling boots, slippers, stockings, corsets, dresses and a parasol for her trousseau. Her trip to California only one month away, she made a trip to Boston in July and

Wedding gown of Mehitable Berry Felton, made in South Danvers, Massachusetts, in 1864, hand-sewn of white silk, alternately striped with organza and satin. *Collection of The Fine Arts Museums of San Francisco.*

The gown was made before Mehitable's arduous journey to California and marriage in San Francisco. Sadly for Mehitable, she was never to wear this gown. The day after her arrival in the west, at 1 p.m. on September 17, 1864, Mehitable was married to James L. Sperry. She wore her gray traveling suit for the ceremony; her gown remained folded in her trunk.

bought twenty yards of "little striped silk" for her white wedding gown. Earlier that month she had bought fourteen yards of taffeta for the petticoat. Her wedding trousseau was completed (from her diary it appears there were sewing ladies assisting) and packed into her trunk, in anticipation of her fashionable San Francisco fall wedding. But when Mehitable arrived in San Francisco after nearly a month of seasickness and after thirteen long years of engagement, she did not unpack. Her plans of a fashionable white wedding had to be changed. She was in the west now; the dress of the east was terribly impractical. Besides, her intended simply could not wait to be married any longer. Instead of the soft, silken gown of Mehitable's dreams, she wore her "grey traveling suit" when she was "married by Dr. Wadsworth at 1 P.M.," the day after her arrival.[108]

Not only was white impractical to the point of being ridiculous in the west, it had also become extravagant, if not unobtainable, in the south during the years of the Civil War. Nevertheless, many a Confederate young woman had dreamed of her own gorgeous white wedding. She knew she could be married in white only once in her lifetime; it was tragically unfortunate that her wedding had to be during such grim, hard times. Still, she sought to have the proper southern wedding in spite of all obstacles.

Cloth was scarce in the south in the summer of 1865 when Louisa McCord was to be married. But she had dreamed of her wedding and of being married in white ever since she could remember; she was determined not to be disappointed. Louisa did have her wish, but not without great sacrifice: "The dress, ten yards of white organdy, was the only piece of white goods in Columbia and was owned by a Yankee shop-keeper who wanted $10.00 in greenbacks for it. To gratify my ardent wish, the last piece of carpet was sold; the chairs from my mother's bedroom, and some lard & butter from the plantation, & the dress was bought."[109]

Other southern brides also wore white, but not newly made, stylish gowns. They wore the altered gowns of their mothers or relatives. For many a young woman, the Civil War forced an early, quick wedding, just before her sweetheart left for duty or hours before having to leave their homes to escape the advances of the Union Army. In Charleston, South Carolina, at the beginning of the war, Frances Ann Hardcastle did not have time to have a white dress made; nor could she have a large wedding. Instead she was married in the brown plaid, silk taffeta dress that she already had.

In New Orleans, Marse Green's household was in a state of panic. Everybody knew the city had fallen, and "it was only a matter of time when his [General Benjamin Franklin Butler's] rule would reach" their town. Always doing things "by fits and starts," Marse Green had announced that morning to his daughters "that they must be ready by early dawn the following day to move themselves and everything else they might need to his plantation on the Amite." But then his dilemma: Fanny's sweetheart, the Captain, was with them, wounded. He would be captured if left behind in his condition; yet he could not go on with the girls — *unless* Fanny and he were married. That being the only solution, the wedding was planned for the same evening. With that announcement, there was "a scene of confusion beyond words to express.... Dear Fanny must be married in white, so every one declared. Then

High-fashion wedding gown, *Peterson's Magazine*, November 1883.

On the left: Wedding dress, 1858, of tissue silk taffeta. *Collection of Amherst Museum Colony Park, Amherst, New York.* On the right: Two-piece wedding gown, c. 1880, silk taffeta. *Collection of the author.*

ensued a ransacking of [already packed] trunks and drawers for a pretty white lawn she had — somewhere! At length it was brought to light in a very crumpled condition, not having been worn since the winter." There was no time, opportunity or place, apparently, to press the gown; Fanny would have to wear it as it was. Then there was a "frantic search for white stockings. Nobody had the temerity to mention white kid gloves. They were of the past, as completely as a thousand other necessities [they] had learned to do without."[110]

At least Fanny actually owned a white dress of her own. There were many other young women who had to create their wedding gowns ingeniously out of the heavy, faded curtains that had blocked the hot afternoon sun for as long as they could remember.

The southern newspapers of the day printed all kinds of helpful articles "on ingenious methods for making something out of nothing." To give her dress that huge southern bell circle, her hoops would be out of oak. Persimmon seeds would have to serve as buttons down her bodice. Her wedding bonnet might be of rice straw or cornshucks; her gloves, the silk stockings she had long ago worn through in the feet. She could not even wear graceful shoes of leather — "the army had first claim."[111] Her shoes, for the most important day of her life, were made of such things as squirrel skin with embarrassingly clumsy wooden soles.

It was wartime and her beloved was on leave for only a short time, maybe just long enough for them to be married. Her only keepsake was not a fine jeweled brooch, but instead a precious golden lock of his hair for inside her "palm leaf broach."[111]

At this same time in Texas, women also were having to concoct their wedding attire in unusual ways, not because of the war but because they lived on the frontier. Coming from the east, they also wanted their wedding gowns to "bell fashionably," but out west they could not buy hoops. For the desired effect, these young woman "set tucks in the under-petticoats and ran mustang grapevines through them." A child attending a wedding and forced also to wear hoops under her new blue silk dress "slipped away during the ceremony, cut all the tapes, took the hoops to the woodpile, and attacked them with a hatchet." Then "like a punctured toy balloon," she went back to "enjoy the wedding."[112]

Indeed young women in Texas could expect almost any kind of attire at their weddings, from a groom in buckskin to a bride in homespun, calico, silks or satins. For one near-sighted groom, buckskin nearly ruined his wedding: "Birt was stopping at Captain Grumbles', and, having only leather breeches and one pair at that, he hired a Negro to wash them after he retired on the eve of the wedding. Not being dry by morning, Birt drew them on and stood before the fire to dry them, a process which 'set' them to perfection, but when he tried to sit down he couldn't make it; so he had to wet them again and sit while he dried them; consequently, when the thump of the bride's crutches on the floor of the inner room announced the approach of the bridal party, the first objects that met the expectant eyes [were] the knees of the bridgroom's pantaloons performing the part of ushers as it were."[113]

The Industrial Revolution, beginning in the 1870's, finally made it possible for most young women in rural areas to have white wedding gowns if they wanted them. For the first time, they had a choice. Even on remote outposts, a young woman might hope to wear white for her wedding, just as she would certainly have done had she not left the civilized east. Most usually, however, someone else would have purchased the silk for her, as it could be many days' arduous trek to a well-stocked town. Sallie Reynolds' sister, in Fort Worth on her way to the Centennial Exposition in Philadelphia, had picked out the white silk alpaca that Sallie wore at Fort Griffin for her 1876 wedding.

But there was another option open to the bride of the mid-1860's and 1870's. She could finally order silk for her wedding gown, as well as a limited number of ready-made items from advertisements in periodicals and metropolitan newspapers.

Also dressmakers like Madame Sanders of Louisville, Kentucky, and Madame Brown of Kansas City, Kansas, advertised that their establishments made gowns to order. While on a cattle drive to Kansas, a man might order

Wedding party, c. 1900, Baja California. *Collection of the Arizona Historical Society, Tucson.*

Fashionable wedding veils, *Godey's Lady's Book and Magazine*, May 1868.

Mail-order advertisement from *Godey's Lady's Book and Magazine*, October 1886, p. 394.

the latest professionally made gown to be sent to his distant ranch when completed.

But relying on the mails could lead to disappointment and disaster. One young bride waited and waited for her gown to come from Houston. Finally it arrived one month late; "the package, sent by express, had been so long enroute that it was worn through and the fabric was frayed."[114]

Since the 1850's, *Godey's Lady's Book* and *Peterson's Magazine* had included diagrams of pattern pieces in miniature, but by 1865 one could actually order patterns from *Godey's*.

At the same time Ebenezer Butterick, a tailor, began advertising and selling by mail his patterns "graded in size, notched, and cut of tissue paper."[115] The McCall Pattern Company followed in 1870. Now, along with her new sewing machine, fine factory-made silk and some patterns to follow, she could make her white bridal gown as fine as anybody's.

Surprisingly, even though most brides had their choice as to their bridal gowns by the last quarter of the nineteenth century, they often as not chose to be married in a fashionable best dress, usually the stylish walking dress, or a two- or three-piece suit in dark blues, greens or browns of the latest fancy goods: heavy, loaded silks, satins, brocades and velvets. Ruth Taylor remembers that her mother, Grace Ford Cook, "wore a gray dress trimmed in black beads" for her home wedding in Gower, Missouri, in 1887. She added, "I think her father had it made. He was a Baptist minister. She was only 16."[116]

The year before Grace's wedding, in 1886, she could have read in *Godey's* that "the most popular colors are navy blue and brown," as well as "plain velvets, also repped or *èpingte* [sic] in cross stripes alternating with plain velvet. . . . Ribbons, feathers and, alas! birds, are the trimmings most popular."[117] Lizzie May Bradford's wedding, two years earlier in Bennington, Vermont, was even ahead of that style. She wore a dress of "satin brocade, with court train, trimmed with ostrich feather trimmings, the entire front

Lizzie May Bradford in her wedding gown, 1884, Bennington, Vermont. *Photograph courtesy of The Bennington Museum, Bennington, Vermont.*
As described in *The Bennington Banner*, February 21, 1884, Lizzie's wedding with more than fifty family and friends present was at her mother's home. Immediately after "a rich collation" in the dining room, Lizzie and her new husband, Chester J. Reynolds, "departed on the five o'clock train for Chicago, which city is to be their home."

being of pearl passimentrie and fringe; the neck cut in square pompadore, and ornamented with a humming bird in one corner, and a pin of twelve diamonds, the latter being the gift of the bridegroom."[118] And Lizzie and her fiancé were married at the Methodist Episcopal Church, following the growing trend toward church weddings.

Certainly, by the end of the nineteenth century, wedding gowns and fashions in general were becoming more and more ostentatious. The bride's trousseau was requiring "at least $200."[119] Lady Jane Rockwell,[120] daughter of Lucy Ann McElroy and Captain Ell B. Rockwell, spent much more than that for her wedding trousseau in 1905. In fact, her wedding was the biggest social event ever in Alburg, Vermont. Lady Jane had spent months planning, shopping and ordering for her trousseau. Nothing had been forgotten: from her starched, white cotton pantaloons, trimmed in deep lace with pink satin ribbons woven through, her delicate lace chemise, her three, fairy-tale-like petticoats, one of them with delicate hearts of lace inserted into the ruffle around the bottom, to the sheer, soft, ice-blue, lace-trimmed long silk slip that would cover everything, making a smooth line for her bridal gown. Her shoes and above-the-elbow, soft white deerskin gloves were from Paris. Everything was new and of the latest, most elegant fashion, except for her handmade cotton "wedding stockings." They were carefully darned and restored for Jane's wedding so that she might wear something old. They were indeed old: an aunt (?) had worn them nearly one hundred years earlier.[121]

Contrasting with the great expenses for Lady Jane's trousseau, in Richford, Vermont, Maud Dinsmore made everything she needed for only $49.15. She was very proud of that, so proud that she wrote a letter to the *Richford Gazette* in 1883, telling how clever she was:

For my wedding dress, I have a very pretty silver-gray silk of light texture. It contains fifteen yards at 60 cents a yard. . . . The tiny pearl buttons cost 50 cents, and the very dainty lace for neck and sleeves, $1. A bonnet to wear with it cost 23 cents for the frame, which I covered with a piece of silk and quilled inside some yellow

---

A portion of Jane Mabel Rockwell's wedding trousseau, with her wedding invitation. *Collection of the author.*
"Lady Jane" was the daughter of the highly esteemed Lake Champlain captain Ell B. Rockwell. Therefore, her wedding to Charles Fuller Carpenter, on August 22, 1905, was a great event in Alburg, Vermont.
In 1984, everything from Jane's wedding day, including her stockings, deerskin shoes, parasol, handbag, gloves and wedding invitation, as well as the wedding gown of her mother, Lucy Ann McElroy Rockwell, was discovered in a trunk in a forgotten attic in the stone tavern in Alburg.

Two-piece wedding suit, 1898, of bengaline and velvet-embossed silk bengaline, and silk. *Collection of Amherst Museum Colony Park, Amherst, New York.*

oriental lace which cost me 50 cents. A bunch of blush roses for the side and silver gray satin ribbon for the strings each cost 50 cents. My light gray gloves cost me $1.25 and have six buttons. My wedding attire . . . therefore amounts to $12.73.

I have sufficient underclothing to last me for two years, four new dresses, three wrappers, three bonnets, three pairs of gloves, and I think a simple but serviceable trousseau for a girl in my position.[122]

No matter the style or the readily available white bridal gown at the end of the nineteenth century, the bride of rural America was generally sensible and practical first. For most, buying a white bridal gown to wear only one time was "wasteful."[123] A best dress, maybe even the dress she already had, would do just fine.

Brides-to-be could follow the proper etiquette for the wedding ceremony from such books as *The Art of Good Behavior* published in 1848:

Cards of invitation are issued, at least a week before hand. The hour selected is usually 8 o'clock, P.M.

Those who belong to the Episcopal and Roman Catholic Churches are usually married at Church, in the morning, and by the prescribed forms. . . . Among other denominations, the parties are married by a clergyman or magistrate, and in the state of New York, marriage being considered by the law only a civil contract, it may be witnessed by any person.

When the hour for the ceremony has arrived, and all things are ready, the wedding party, consisting of the happy couple, with the bridesmaids and groomsmen, walk into the room arm in arm; the groomsmen each attending the bridesmaids, preceding the bride and bridegroom, and take their position at the head of the room, which is usually the end farthest from the entrance; the bride standing facing the assembly on the right of the bridegroom — the bridesmaids taking their position at her right, and the groomsmen at the left of the bridegroom. The principal groomsman now formally introduces the clergyman or magistrate to the bride and bridegroom, and he proceeds to perform the marriage ceremony: if a ring is to be used, the bridegroom procures a plain gold one previously, taking some means to have it of the proper size.

As soon as the ceremony is over, and the bridegroom has kissed the bride, the clergyman or magistrate shakes hands with the bride, saluting her by her newly acquired name, as Mrs. —, and wishes them joy, prosperity and happiness: the groomsmen and bridesmaids then do the same; and then the principal groomsman brings to them the other persons in the room, commencing with the parents and relatives of the parties, the bride's relations having precedence, and ladies being accompanied by gentlemen.

When the presentations and congratulations are over, . . . the bridal party, which, till now, has kept its position, mingles with the rest of the company, and joins in the dancing or other amusements. The festivities should not be kept up too late; and at the hour of retiring the bride is to be conducted to the bridal chamber by the bridesmaids, who assist her in her night-toilette. The bridegroom upon receiving notice will retire, without farther attendance or ceremony.

The chamber frolics, such as the whole company visiting the bride and bridegroom after they were in bed, which was done some years ago, even at the marriage of monarchs, and the custom of throwing the stocking, etc. are almost universally laid aside.[124]

A late-nineteenth-century wedding invitation. *Gift of Barbara Chiolino to the author.*

WEDDING PARTY

Flower girl
   She strews petals of flowers in front of the bride, symbolizing fertility.

Bridesmaids
   In primitive marriages, the couple was surrounded by many other young people dressed similarly so that the evil spirits could not distinguish which was the bridal pair. For this reason, bridesmaids are dressed alike.

Best man
   He goes back to the days of marriage by capture when he would wait and watch for the moment when the bride could be taken, helping the groom with the actual capture.

One New Englander wrote of the early nineteenth century,

Justices were almost universally employed to perform the marriage ceremony, and the marriage fee was one dollar; and the officiating magistrate was considered very penurious if he did not make a present of that dollar to the bride; and in many cases an amount of flax was purchased with that dollar and manufactured into linen for family use. . . . I recollect in one instance, in performing the marriage ceremony the justice and the father of the bride having a relish for gin and having imbibed freely of that cordial previous to the ceremony, when the happy couple presented themselves ready for the ceremony with their gloves on, the justice required them to remove their gloves, as his custom was to marry *skin to skin.*[125]

But at the time this man was writing (in the 1870's to 1880's), the ceremony had changed: it was no longer "considered respectable . . . to have a marriage solemnized by a justice. These rites must be performed by the pastor or some noted clergyman, and $10 dollars is considered a moderate marriage fee."[125]

Of course, out on the western frontier all rules and laws were flexible and

This Certifies

That Mr. John J. Rohman AND Miss Ella A. Augspurger
of Hamilton, of Middletown,
State of Ohio. State of Ohio.

were by me united

IN HOLY MATRIMONY

According to the ORDINANCE OF GOD
And the Laws of the State of
Ohio

At Trenton on the 15th day of November
In the year of our LORD, one thousand eight hundred
and ninety nine.

Witnesses.

Rev. H. J. Krehbiel

And Boaz took Ruth, and she was his wife.
Ruth 4:13

Marriage Certificate of Mr. John J. Rohman and Miss Ella A. Augspurger, November 15, 1899, in Trenton, Ohio.
Collection of the author, a great-granddaughter of the couple.

often changed altogether. Many times even the date of the wedding depended on whenever the Methodist circuit rider or Baptist minister might ride into the settlement. In the west "Protestant ministers . . . were few [and the words] were usually spoken by a Jesuit missionary . . . or by some justice of the peace of doubtful powers and mythical appointment." When one of those could not be found, the father of the bride sometimes took it upon himself to marry the couple with the understanding that they be properly joined as soon as the first minister came through. Sometimes many months elapsed, but "no scandal ever arose — the marriage vow was never broken."[126]

Although only by word of mouth, news of a wedding celebration traveled quickly, even several days' journey away. Anyone who heard the announcement was welcome; consequently, people rode great distances to a "neighbor" they had never met, the wedding festivities being an excuse for a break in their daily toil and loneliness.

And one could never predict the locale of a frontier wedding ceremony beforehand. There was not always space inside the dugout or sod house on the plains; instead, the wedding might be on the porch, the clutter of horses, buggies, men, women and children coloring the otherwise monotonous, vast expanses of treeless prairie.

A solution to no house at all was a buggy wedding. The bride and groom repeated their vows seated inside the buggy while family and neighbors gathered around. With the reins in his hands, the groom was free to drive off into the sun, or sunset, as soon as the minister had pronounced them man and wife. The bride could only reach out in futile last good-byes as the buggy hurried off to some isolated abode in the distance.

No matter the part of the country, however, most weddings still took place at the bride's house. Even Davy Crockett in Tennessee ended up being married at his girl's house despite his dead-set determination against it. He had thought he could not be married there after his girl's mother ("the old lady," as Davy referred to her) looked on him "as savage as a meat axe" when he had "broached the subject" of marriage the previous week. As he recounted his wedding day:

When I arrived I never pretended to dismount from my horse, but rode up to the door, and asked the girl if she was ready; and she said she was. I then told her to

WEDDING RING

With this ring I wed thee,
With this gold and silver I honour thee,
With this gift I dowe thee.
— English

Its circular shape represents the imperishable covenant of marriage, the everlasting promise.

Never buy a wedding ring on Friday or by mail, as it is bad luck if another person has

tried it on. Never try on the ring before marriage or you will never marry. Never drop the ring in the ceremony; the person who drops it will be the first to die. If the ring should ever break, there will be a quarrel or separation.

The ring finger is the fourth finger of the left hand because it was believed that "from thence there proceeds a particular vein to the heart. . . . They thought this finger the

properest to bear this pledge of love, that from thence it might be conveyed, as it were, to the heart." The fourth finger is also the least active finger of the hand, so that the ring would be displayed and not wear out. William Tegg, The Knot Tied: Marriage Ceremonies of All Nations *(Detroit: Singing Tree Press, 1970), p. 26.*

A Hopi bride with her wedding bundle, 1901, Oraibi Pueblo, Hopi, Arizona. *Collection of the Museum of New Mexico (Negative number 37544). Photograph by Carl N. Werntz.*
The bride is wearing her white cotton wedding robe over a new blue or black dress. Supplied mostly by the bridegroom, the raw cotton of her wedding costume was carded, spun and woven by the men of the family into her belt, a large and a small wedding robe.
The bride carries her large wedding robe and belt inside her reed bundle, the long fringe with tassels purposely hanging down the sides of the bundle to symbolize fertilizing rain.

light on the horse I was leading; and she did so. Her father, though, had gone out to the gate, and when I started he commenced persuading me to stay and marry there; that he was entirely willing to the match, and that his wife, like most women, had entirely too much tongue; but that I oughtn't to mind her. I told him if she would ask me to stay and marry at her house, I would do so. With that he sent for her, and after they had talked for some time out by themselves, she came to me and looked at me mighty good, and asked my pardon for what she had said, and invited me to stay. She said it was the first child she had ever had to marry; and she couldn't bear to see her go off in that way; that if I would light, she would do the best she could for us. I couldn't stand every thing, and so I agreed, and we got down, and went in. I sent off then for my parson, and got married in a short time; for I was afraid to wait long, for fear of another defeat. We had as good treatment as could be expected.[127]

At another wedding "far up in the wilds of New Hampshire, . . . all was as silent as the house of mourning" as the marriage ceremony was to begin:

After a few minutes, during which not a word, even in a whisper, was uttered, the parties to be joined in lawful wedlock entered the room, arm in arm. . . . They passed along, curving with the circle in their progress, until they came opposite to the lights upon the wall, when, wheeling about, they stood bolt upright, waiting for the parson to begin.[128]

The minister rose, and with him the people. A short and appropriate prayer was made, to which several responsive amens were uttered, when the clergyman requested the certificate of publishment. . . . The bridegroom, after fumbling unsuccessfully in several pockets, recollected that he had left it in his hat, and started off to obtain it. The bride, meanwhile, stood waiting, unembarrassed by the crowd, the occasion, or the awkwardness of her partner's absence. The former soon returned, and handing it to the clergyman, resumed his place. After casting his eyes over the paper, crumpled and soiled almost to the point of illegibility, the service recommenced.[129]

The clergyman asked that the bridegroom "take the woman by the right hand. . . . After a brief exhortation on the solemnity of the act, and the responsibilities and obligations of married life, the clergyman, asking each party to repeat the vows, pronounced them man and wife; and supposing his duties discharged, sat down." But the bride and groom did not move. Finally the host yelled out, "She's waiting for you to buss her, parson!" With that the

One stereoscopic image, entitled "The Wedding March," of an elaborate big-city wedding, c. 1880–1900. *Collection of the author.*

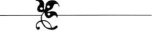

CERTIFICATE OF MARRIAGE.

THIS IS TO CERTIFY,

That, on the _____ day of _____ 18 66
Mr. J. E. Fellows of Albion Pa and
Miss A. C. Bradish of Albion Pa were
by me joined in Marriage. Given at _____ this
1st day of _____ 1866

Henry E. Ball
Justice of the Peace

OBSERVER PRINT, ERIE.

Certificate of Marriage, Mr. J. E. Fellows to Miss A. C. Bradish, January 1, 1866, both of Albion, Pennsylvania. *Collection of the author.*
Here is a wedding in the "proper style." It is not yet fashionable for the bride to wear her veil over her face. She carries a handkerchief for her tears. Right hands are clasped as the bride and groom repeat their vows.

parson rose and kissed the bride, then shook the hands of the bridegroom. Everyone followed, "the men kissing the bride, the women being kissed by the bridegroom." According to one observer, there was so much kissing that "the noise, repeated and re-repeated, in every part of the room, reminded [him] of nothing so much as an irregular volley of small-arms at a militia muster."[130]

In Springfield, Illinois, Mary Todd and Abraham Lincoln's last-minute ceremony on November 4, 1842, was held in front of the fireplace with two oil lamps on the mantel with "not more than thirty people ... present." Mary had three bridesmaids but "'no one stood up with' Lincoln — 'Just he and Mary stood up alone.'"[131]

"There was of course a perfect hush in the room as the ceremony progressed." Dr. Dresser began the Episcopal marriage service, "Dearly beloved, we are gathered together here in the sight of God, and in the face of this company, to join together this Man and this Woman in holy Matrimony." Their right hands were joined as Abraham repeated after the minister, "I Abraham take thee Mary to my wedded Wife, to have and to hold from this day forward, for better for worse, for richer for poorer, in sickness and in health, to love and to cherish, till death us do part ... and thereto I plight thee my troth."[132] Mary repeated the vows after the minister.

But then, "The Parson handed Lincoln the ring, and as he put it on the

BRIDAL HANDKERCHIEF

The elaborately worked bridal handkerchief was an important item in the bride's attire, the old saying being, "A bride weeps on her wedding day, or tears will fall later."

Lithograph from *Harper's Weekly*, June 30, 1866, entitled "Marriage of a Colored Soldier at Vicksburg by Chaplain Warren of the Freedmen's Bureau." *Collection of Mississippi Department of Archives and History, Jackson.*
The bride is wearing a fashionable white wedding gown and veil. "If clothes served to announce a woman's awareness of her new status, they also revealed the change in male-female relationships from slave unions to legal marriages. Black husbands took pride in buying fashionable dresses . . . for their womenfolk. When a freedman walked alongside his well-dressed wife, both partners dramatized the legitimacy of their relationship and his role as family provider." (Jacqueline Jones, *Labor of Love, Labor of Sorrow: Black Women, Work, and the Family from Slavery to the Present* [New York: Vintage Books, 1985], p. 69.)

brides finger, went through the church formula, 'With this ring I thee endow with all my goods and chattels, lands and tenements.'" Just then, Lincoln's friend Judge Thomas Brown, standing behind him, blurted out, "'Lord Jesus Christ, God Almighty, Lincoln, the Statute fixes all that.'. . . The Old Parson . . . broke down under it — an almost irresistable desire to laugh out, checked his proceding [sic] for a minute or so — but finally recovered and pronounced them Husband & wife."[133]

At Fanny's hurried New Orleans marriage ceremony during the Civil War, the Methodist preacher could not be found; an Episcopal minister would have to do. With neighbors all assembled to give the bride away, "Mr. McHatton volunteered to perform that function. . . . Somebody produced a plain gold ring, which, no doubt, was afterwards returned with appropriate thanks." Quickly Fanny and the Captain "with a bandaged head and...ill-fitting clothes, not even store-made," were married. "Their healths were drunk in tepid lemonade." Then there were congratulations and good-byes, as well as a "God bless you!" and a kiss from one neighbor who had to hurry back to her two wounded brothers at home.[134]

For the Quaker couple, like Dolly Payne and John Todd, the marriage ceremony was in a "bare-walled meeting house...with neither priest nor chanting choir." Dolly and John

stood up together upon the "women's side" and declared before God, and the assembled Society, their intention of taking each other as husband and wife...: "I, John Todd, do take thee Dorothea Payne to be my wedded wife, and promise, through divine assistance, to be unto thee a loving husband, until separated by death."[135]

Then Dolly repeated the vow; the certificate of marriage was read, and the register was signed by all the witnesses.

Wedding photograph of Nannie and John Ward, c. 1875, taken in Brownsville, Pennsylvania. *Collection of the author.*

When the wedding ceremony was over, there were always festivities, varying in different parts of the country. In New England, "A newly married couple was not 'treated right' unless they were given a serenade." "When a couple got married they were honored by all hands in the neighborhood. . . . Everyone carried a noise maker of some kind. It might be a musical instrument or just anything which could make a noise — the louder the better. This continued until the bridegroom appeared and invited them in for a feast. At many places they found long tables all set with a plentiful supply of good things to eat. At one place they were not invited in for eats, so went back and serenaded the newly-weds for two nights. No one could possibly sleep while the serenade was in progress. After the first night the hired man said he would go out and help them if they came again, so I suppose he did. On the third night they found some cider 'set out' so they called off going there any more. They probably needed to stay home and get some sleep too."[136]

When Marietta Rice's nearest neighbor, Abner Tolles, was married on March 25, 1862, despite the "terrible war" going on, "the boys serenaded [sic] him good. . . . He invited them in and treated them to apples and cider."[137]

Nearly a week later, Marietta wrote into her diary that they were going to "call upon Abner and his wife" and the next day she penned, "Had a good time at Abners was treated to wedding cake, apples and cider."[138]

One time-consuming preparation for the wedding was cutting the cake into tiny squares about the size of a little finger. Then each piece of cake had to be threaded through the wedding ring. This was done before the ring was ever put on the finger, because once the wedding ring was on, it should never be removed. Then the cakes were wrapped in paper or put into tiny boxes for good-luck gifts, especially for young, unmarried guests.

It was that gift of a tiny piece of wedding cake that was special and exciting to fifteen-year-old Marietta. "It [was] a very common superstition that girls who sleep with a piece of wedding cake under their pillow will dream of their future husbands."[139] Marietta was anxious to dream of her intended, but for her the cake had a surprise result. On April 3, she wrote into her diary, "I have slept 2 nights on my wedding cake, dreamed about someone whose name was not on the paper." The cake no longer under her pillow nor any beau having come forth, several weeks later Marietta was enjoying herself "copying embroidery patterns out of Godey's."[140]

The gift of bridal cake was also important to Mrs. John Quincy Adams. In 1820 she wrote, "I didn't get a bit of cake and Mary had none to dream on." Eight years later, to her son, she again remarked about the cake, "I send you a piece of cake as it is the fashion. Judge Cranch declined taking any as he said old people had 'nothing but dreams' on such occasions."[141]

Albert Britt remembered merrymaking similar to New England's serenading, but in Illinois where he was from they called it "shivaree" (charivari).[142] "A discordant concert of horns, tin pans, shotguns fired in the air, horse fiddles, anything to make a noise," it is no wonder that it was "usually mercifully brief, then the door opened and the makers of the noise trooped into the house to be treated to cigars by the provident groom." Albert Britt added that by definition, "this celebration was aimed only at an unpopular pair and was intended as an insult. It was not so with us."[143]

The festivities of a prosperous German-Russian family in Kansas in 1876 included "eating, drinking and dancing the hoch-zeit. . . . Whiskey was passed around after each dance and the men smoked their long-stem pipes even while they were dancing. Every man danced with the bride, and greenbacks were pinned all over her dress by the guests."[144]

Originating on the frontier, merrymaking was such an important part of weddings in the rural south that the ceremony was held in the morning or at noon in order that there would be hours and hours for celebrating. Having first gathered at the groom's home, the groom's party rode together to the bride's, racing for the bottle all along the way. Of course, it was only considerate that the winner share his prize; thus, by the time the men arrived at the wedding, they were in jovial spirits and ready for a good time.

Early in the afternoon there would be a wedding feast. While still the frontier, this would consist mainly of game depending "upon the luck of the chase." Later, on farms and plantations, however, "the bride's family took pride in the amount [of food] set forth."[145] After the feast, dancing began which often continued until midnight or later. No matter, the bride and groom were not permitted to remain at the festivities. It was the custom for the bride's friends to put her to bed. Then the groom was tucked in beside her

Ethel Golden and Harold Nichols with their wedding party, June 9, 1920. *Photograph courtesy of Harold and Ethel Golden Nichols.*

AN 1833 RECIPE FOR WEDDING CAKE

Good common wedding cake may be made thus: Four pounds of flour, three pounds of butter, three pounds of sugar, four pounds of currants, two pounds of raisins, twenty-four eggs, half a pint of brandy, or lemon-brandy, one ounce of mace, and three nutmegs. A little molasses makes it dark colored, which is desirable. Half a pound of citron improves it; but it is not necessary. To be baked two hours and a half, or three hours. After the oven is cleared, it is well to shut the door for eight or ten minutes, to let the violence of the heat subside, before cake or bread is put in.

To make icing for your wedding cake, beat the whites of eggs to an entire froth, and to each egg add five teaspoonfuls of sifted loaf sugar, gradually; beat it a great while. Put it on when your cake is hot, or cold, as is most convenient. It will dry in a warm room, a short distance from a gentle fire, or in a warm oven.

by his friends. In the morning the wedding party made its way to the groom's house for the infare, where another feast was set forth by his family.

Celebrations for a second marriage were not as elaborate, but there usually would be a shivaree for the newly married couple, keeping them awake with all the noisemaking and rowdiness.

In the southwest there was always candy making, the "candy being made of molasses in a wash pot out in the yard."[146] Then adults and children enjoyed the fun of the candy pull. Every wedding had its fiddle players, improvising the music for square dancing. The fiddler would play all night, the menfolk passing a hat around to pay him.

After Margaret Holden Eaton was married in the groom's sister's house in Santa Barbara, California, her new father-in-law instructed her and Ira to perform "a very old-fashioned custom of the early days." "In front of the whole company," Father Eaton had asked them to stand "one on each side of the parlor door." As Margaret later recorded in her diary, "He had bored a hole over the door and inserted a piece of cotton rope; he handed me one end of the rope and Ira the other. Then he told us to pull as hard as we could to see who was stronger. Of course Ira pulled the rope from me," signifying that "we would always pull together, and that the man should always lead and the woman follow."[147]

For Quakers, following superstitions was forbidden. Also there was no serenading or shivaree to gain entrance to the refreshments. Instead, all who signed the marriage register were to have dinner and later supper at the bride's parents. Understandably it was quite typical for the entire congregation to sign the register; at Dolly Payne and John Todd's marriage, the register included the names of more than seventy people.

No matter religion or location of the wedding, after the ceremony was over "refreshments were passed." Many times they were simple, as at Alexander and Emily Clapp's wedding in 1829 in New England: "they consisted of cake baked in five quart pans in a brisk oven with raisins put in whole and cinnamon added for seasoning, mulled cider, and cheese."[148]

Inside dugouts and sodhouses on the prairies of Kansas, women of the household also prepared delicious wedding suppers, but many times they had to be creative and ingenious, making a feast from little more than bare necessities. Down in her dugout, Mrs. Brown "receive[d] her guests with all the dignity of the first lady of the land." She served them "some delicious coffee, made of dried carrots," freshly ground in her coffee mill, "seven different kinds of sauce, all made out of wild plums put up in seven different ways, . . . plain bread and butter, and fried pork."[149] The minister was paid in potatoes for performing the ceremony.

Southern girls, spoiled by "no lack of provisions" at earlier weddings, had to accept the "imitation" wedding supper during the Civil War. Elizabeth Grisham remembered the great amount of food for her wedding supper in West Union, South Carolina, in 1847, listing "chickens, turkeys, bacon, hams and roast beef in abundance, four fat shoats . . . killed and cooked two of them roasted whole . . . all kinds of fruit pies and custards by the dozens, tea cakes, marvels, jumbles and ginger cakes by the peck and half bushel. Three large steeple cakes, over two feet high, with ornaments on top of each, . . . pound cakes, sponge cakes, fruit cakes, snow balls, matrimony, jellies, nuts, candies, syllabub, boiled custard, coffee, tea, biscuit crackers, light bread and fruits of the season."[150]

Elizabeth and her family "were over two weeks making the cakes. . . . We had a hen's nest made of preserved orange peelings that had been preserved in long strips and then round together in the shape of a large nest. The eggs in the nest were blanc mange that had been shaped in egg shells. The cakes were trimmed with icing, small sugar plums and silver leaf. The fruit cakes with citron cut or trimmed into fancy shapes of leaves, hearts, etc., with gold leaf on them. Some of the melon-shaped cakes were made yellow by putting yellow of egg well beaten over the icing."[150]

Southern brides sadly thought of those beautiful parties, wishing their own table not to be so poor. It was wartime and now they were fortunate to have "a toast of tomato wine, a table with a roasted stray chicken, dried apple pie, blackberry leaf tea and coffee made from okra seeds."[151]

Of course, there were those unfortunate circumstances in which the bride had no wedding supper or celebration at all. Such was the case for Annie E. Osborn. Her intended, Daniel R. Anthony, Susan B. Anthony's brother, had not known when he might expect his sweetheart from New York and had been unable to make wedding preparations ahead. Immediately upon her arrival in Kansas, although late in the evening, Daniel "hired the stagecoach driver to take them to the Rev. S. L. Adair's cabin, where the ceremony was performed with the Adair household witnessing from their beds." Without any wedding supper or cake, Daniel took his new bride to his cabin, "where the bride was greeted by the newly butchered hogs hanging from the rafters, there being no safe place outside to put them."[152]

Annie E. Osborn and Daniel R. Anthony were the exception, for usually, no matter how poor the circumstances, there was cake of some kind at the wedding. According to Mrs. Henry Ward Beecher, the wedding cake went hand-in-hand with the bridal gown: "The wedding-dress and wedding-cake were to be made — for what New England damsel could be married without wedding-cake?"[153]

There was even a wedding cake at Mary Todd and Abraham Lincoln's last-minute wedding. With fear that their marriage would be prevented by Mary's family, the couple had announced their plans to be wed the very morning it was to take place. Thinking they "could not have a festive wedding,

WEDDING CAKE

Originally called bride cake, later bride's cake, the wedding cake has always been an important part of the wedding festivities, with much symbolism. The bridal cake was at weddings since Roman times, then made of grain and salt. In Greece, the cake was of pounded grain and honey. The iced marzipan cake began in the seventeenth century. In early America the typical wedding cake was a dark fruit type that could be stored. By the time of the Civil War, the traditional white wedding cake had appeared. Then two kinds of wedding cake were customary: the dark fruit cake was the groom's cake; the white cake was the bride's. For many brides of the countryside, however, the popular wedding cake was a rich pound cake.

Whatever the kind of cake, there were two very important traditions: the bride must cut the first piece or she would be childless; she must save a piece, no matter if only a crumb, for her and her husband to eat on their first anniversary for luck and a long life together.

Sunburst, made as a wedding present by family and friends for Mary Wait Mather, Weathersfield, Vermont, for her second marriage, 1853, 84½ × 87½ inches, pieced and appliquéd cottons. *Collection of the author.*
The quilt is inscribed with the date "May, 1853." Mary was married on June 1st of that year.

much as Mary would have liked it," they had decided to "go quietly to Dr. Charles Dresser, the Episcopal minister, and have the ceremony at his home."[154] On the morning of November 4, 1842, Lincoln went to Dr. Dresser's home, and interrupting breakfast said, "I want to get hitched tonight." When Mary finally announced her intentions to the Edwardses, she was warned, "Do not forget that you are a Todd."[155] Nevertheless, Abraham and Mary were so determined to be married that her family could not prevent them. After hours of arguments and stress, the family finally decided the wedding must take place at the Edwardses' home. After all, it was only proper. In a rush and panic, preparations were made. The disapproving, frowning women of the household had so little time to make the refreshments that the wedding cake was still warm when it was served.

Guests did not generally bring wedding gifts before the latter part of the nineteenth century. There were several exceptions, however. By the 1840's, family and friends often presented a friendship quilt to the bride. It was a most meaningful and appropriate gift, even practical with all their names, many times all the information needed to write to them, a nineteenth-century directory. When Mary Mather was married to Samuel Steel on June 1, 1853, in Weathersfield, Vermont, amidst all the merrymaking, her neighbors and family gave her the quilt they had finished only days earlier. This was not an ordinary friendship quilt made up of a common, simple block. Family and friends had chosen the twenty-four-point *Sunburst* pattern for "Mrs. M's" quilt. It was an unusual quilt for an unusual wedding, for this was Mary's second marriage. All the women were so happy for her. Only someone as sweet and attractive as Mary could ever hope to re-marry again, she having three small boys yet to provide for. Indeed, men remarried quickly when they were widowers with little ones, but widows with children could expect to live out their days as widows. Perhaps, since Mary would be moving away, the most poignant block was from Mary's dearest friend and neighbor's daughter, Susan Tenney. She had penned

To Mrs. M —
Remember all who love Thee
And all who are loved by Thee
Ascutneyville
Vt.
May 1853

A bridal friendship quilt was the gift of women to the bride, but a traditional gift given to both the bride and the groom was a pair of cedar trees to be planted on either side of the front door of the couple's new home. The trees were evergreens, representing long-lasting life and marriage. Also throughout the century, it was traditional to decorate the church or home for the wedding with branches or wreaths of evergreens.

Until the mid-nineteenth century, a father gave his daughter some type of a dowry to take to her new home, a custom going back to marriage by purchase. In 1720 Judith Sewall received a wedding outfit befitting a wealth-

WEDDING FAVORS

Knots were one of the earliest forms of marriage. Literally the couple's clothes were tied together with a knot, from whence the expression "tying the marriage knot" originated. Thus, knots of ribbons were given as favors, at first of bright colors. Then, by the eighteenth century, they could only be white; simply the "vulgar" continued to give the colored ones.

Gloves were given as wedding favors. The verse often accompanying the gloves was "Take away the 'g' and make us a pair of loves."

A piece of wedding cake first threaded through the bride's ring a certain number of times (popularly nine times) was a most important favor. If it were put into the left stocking and then under the pillow, one could expect dreams of his or her future marriage partner.

ier New England family: "A Duzen of good Black Walnut Chairs, A Duzen Cane Chairs, and a great chair for a chamber, all black Walnut. One Duzen large Pewter Plates, new fashion, a Duzen Ivory-hafted knives and forks. Four Duzen small glass salt cellars, Curtain and Vallens for a Bed with Counterpane, Head Cloth, and Tester made of good yellow watered camlet with Trimming.... A good fine larger Chintz quilt, well made."[156] Every item, including the "Chintz quilt" and additional kitchen items, was ordered from England.

In 1790 Aaron Guild was very generous in the dowry to his first married daughter. He gave her over nine pounds in cash, a "chest with draws, nine chairs, a fall leaf table, a kitchen table, two beds and bedsteads, one pair of

Mary Elizabeth Steel (front left), a sister (behind) and her mother (?), Mary Wait Mather Steel (right). *Photograph courtesy of Ina Adams.*

86

Town clerk's record of the marriage of Mr. Samuel Steele [sic] to Mrs. Mary C. Mather, June 1, 1853. *Marriage Records, Town Clerk's Office, Weathersfield, Vermont.*

cotton sheets, three pair of tow sheets, Twenty-two yards of diaper, One Coverled, two Wheels, Tub and Churn, Bread trough and pail, Shovel & tongs & tost iron, One pot & pair of Dogs, Teakittle, One dish kittle one spider and skillet pair of flat irons, Boiling brass kittle & dish Kittle and One cow." [157]

Nancy Batchelder's "setting out" from her parents in 1840 was more typical: a spinning wheel and the bedding and linens she would need "carefully calculated" by her mother, as well as six sheep and the traditional gift of a cow. Nancy wrote, "this was my outfit." [158]

In St. Albans, Vermont, a good wedding present consisted of "six wooden or pewter plates, with spoons to match, a cooking pot, *and always a cradle;* and it was a lucky bride who received a spinning-wheel and a side-saddle." [159]

When Davy Crockett went back to his "old Irish mother" a few days after having married her daughter, he found her in "the finest humour in the world." He wrote, "She gave us two likely cows and calves, which, though it was a small marriage-portion, was still better than I had expected, and, indeed, it was about all I ever got." [160]

Of course, for some there were very elaborate wedding gifts. The day after Senator Stephen A. Douglas of Illinois married Martha Martin of North Carolina, "Robert Martin handed his new son-in-law a deed to the Pearl River plantations with all their equipment and slaves." This included over three thousand acres of "fertile bottomland with easy access to the New Orleans market by way of the Pearl River," including a cotton gin, a cane mill and a boat landing for the shipment of cotton. Believed to have been "motivated more by political considerations than moral ones," Douglas did not accept it: "as a Northern man by birth, education, and residence, he was totally ignorant of plantation management." He is said, however, to have "suggested to his father-in-law that, were it to be willed to his wife Martha, he could not refuse it." [161]

THROWING RICE

Supposedly from the primitive urge to throw things at the bride, the Hebrews threw cake, the Greeks threw grain, fruit and sweetmeats, all symbolic of best wishes for fertility.

Later flowers and petals were thrown at the bride and groom. By the 1870's, rice was used.

87

Daguerreotype of a young married couple, mid-nineteenth century. *Collection of the author.*

Wedding celebrations did not end on the wedding day but went on sometimes for weeks. The "infare," or reception at the groom's home, was usually on the second day. Sallie Reynolds Matthews wrote of one in Texas:

Mother did not go to the wedding but stayed at home to make ready the reception of the little bride. In this she was helped by a friend and former neighbor. . . . There was much roasting and baking. . . . The wedding party came in on the afternoon of the third day, having spent the night at the Stockton Ranch on the way. They were all on horseback and came riding in by twos, with the Newcombs leading, the bride and groom next, followed by some six or eight other couples. There were three fiddlers in the party, one having been hired to play for the dance. He became tired around twelve o'clock and quit the job and went to bed, but another took his place and they danced on until break of day, with plenty of coffee and cake to keep them going, the coffee being made in a sizable wash pot and kept hot over the coals in the fireplace.[162]

Also it was traditional that days were set aside to visit the bride and groom, perhaps every Wednesday for a month. In New England, the bride held a special place in the community for as long as a month of Sundays. The custom then was known as "coming out bride." From New England throughout the south, on the first Sunday after the wedding and for as many as four Sundays after that, no matter their ages, the bride and groom "went to the church services dressed with as much pretty, and distinctly bridal, finery as was their good hap to possess." Purposefully a little late so as to capture everyone's attention, the newlyweds paraded arm-in-arm down the aisle of the meeting house, taking the most prominent place in the congregation. Then, "usually after the singing of the second hymn, the happy couple, in agonies of shyness and pride, rose to their feet, and turned slowly twice or thrice around before the eyes of the whole delighted assembly, thus displaying to the full every detail of their attire."[163]

For little Sarah Anna Emery, that was very memorable. She "had been considered too young to attend the [wedding] party, but . . . saw Madam Woods the next Sunday. She 'walked out bride,' in a green silk dress, a white satin bonnet, a white satin cardinal, trimmed with white fur, and a grey fox muff and tippet. She was a tall, handsome lady."[164]

Not all "coming out brides" were able to put on such a show. In June of 1840, Anne Langton was disappointed in one: "The bride was in church, and as she wore white gloves, I suppose it was considered a formal appearance, though most informal it appeared, as she sat on one bench and her husband several benches behind her. She was dressed in a rich drab silk, with fancy straw, or chip bonnet, and white ribbons."[165] But the next week she wrote, "The bride (Mrs. Wallis) Looked much better than on the Sunday of her first appearance. Her dress was of another shade, richer than the former. I think it would have stood erect by itself."[166]

*S*uddenly the new bride emerged out of all the magical excitement of her wedding and the festivities as wife in her new married life. The fun, the merriment of her girlhood years were over. She was a bride for one glorious moment; she was married for the rest of her life and must put on the maturity appropriate for this place in life. Many a new bride was unexpectedly shocked to find herself away from family and friends, literally everyone she ever knew, in totally intolerable surroundings, to be with a man she might know only from formal Saturday-night visits. And what a shock for some new brides at the

transformation worked in a lover after marriage. . . . Before the nuptial knot is tied, the suitor is all devotion. No business engagement is permitted to infringe on the evenings consecrated to his finance [sic]. If she drops her fan, misplaces a glove, or needs help in putting on her shawl, he is instantly at her side, the most eager, the most patient, the most delicate of servants. She has only to express a wish to go to church, or to visit some place of amusement, and lo! he waits on her even before breakfast, though it rains as if a deluge had come. But when the irrevocable vows are said and the honeymoon comfortably over, a change too often comes over the obsequious cavalier. The latent selfishness begins to develope itself. The wife has to pick up her own fan, search for her own gloves, shawl herself unassisted, go to church alone.[167]

In "The School-Mistress Married," in *Godey's* in January of 1854, a young bride expressed her grief at having given up teaching for marriage:

THROWING THE BOUQUET
AND GARTER

This grew out of the popular custom of "flinging the stocking" of the eighteenth century. After the bride and bridegroom were put to bed, the entire wedding party joined them in the room. The men then took the bride's stockings, the women those of the bridegroom. Seated at the foot of the bridal bed, they took turns trying to fling the stockings "backward, o'er head . . . to hit him or her on the nose." As the superstition went,
Who hits the mark o'er the left shoulder
Must married be ere twelve months older.
(Progress of Matrimony, 1733)
Today there is a variation with the bouquet or garter: the bride or bridegroom throws it over the shoulder to the same sex; with the stockings, the women had to hit the bridegroom; the men had to hit the bride.

Oh, for *my* little school-room, *my* green benches, *my* two *cracked* bricks!!!
    Now, girls, accept of a little advice,
"Experience teaches one how to be wise."
A year or two since, I would fall in love;
Of all men created, below or above,
    There was never another.
A man *so* endowed with every perfection,
That even mamma no sort of objection
    Could find to my lover.

We married, the horror of all to endure!
Somewhat of a hubbub was kicked up, be sure;
There was cake to be cut and evenly lie,
And white satin ribbon in bow knots to tie,
    And notes to be written.
And dresses sent out and brought home,
And callers unwelcome would come,
    And sit, and keep sitting.

The groom was, as *usual*, a little *too late* —
Procrastination, of *all* things, I hate! —
His cravat, *then*, was tied in a great crooked bow.
Our trunks must be packed, all ready to go —
    I was no more a teacher.

Now, girls, these *faint* facts in time you may know,
And moan that in youth you did not bestow
More note on these lines, in sympathy penned
To advise you; and oh, you will need a friend!
    For I *know* you *will* marry.[168]

THROWING CONFETTI

Originally this was tiny sweetmeats of sugared almonds thrown by the crowd at festivals in Italy. In Paris, confetti was made of pellets of plaster, but they were so dangerous that they were replaced by paper. In the nineteenth century the pieces of paper were cut into tiny symbols. Later they became small circles of colored tissue paper.

THROWING SHOES

Considered the owner's life essence, shoes were thrown after the couple for good luck. They also represented the transference of authority from the father to the husband.

   In the eighteenth and nineteenth centuries, satin slippers were thrown at the carriage as the bridal pair were driving off. The superstition was that a slipper alighting on the top of the carriage promised good luck forever.

"Like most young ladies, [Bessie] had at times been impatient of restraint, but had consoled herself with the idea, that when she was married, all trouble would be left behind. She could then go where she liked, do what she liked, and no one would have a right to control or say to her, 'why do you so?'" But as a new bride "she commenced housekeeping in the old house near the school-house, where she had spent so many days of her childhood; and the scouring of the yellow-pine floor devolved upon her." [169]

Of absolute necessity, a bride brought with her all the linens, sheets and pillowcases, as well as quilts, blankets and coverlets she needed when she was married. From then on she would have to card, spin, weave, sew and mend all of the clothing, as well as knit and darn the stockings, caps and mittens worn by her husband and children. She would have to do that every working day of her adult life as long as she was physically able. There would be no time after her marriage to make the great amounts of yardage for everyday bed linens.

Traditionally, she need bring a dozen of each item, including a dozen quilts. Those quilts would most likely provide the only decoration within her otherwise drab surroundings. In addition it was important for a bride to take with her a best quilt, her bride's quilt. Sarah Hoisington Richardson made an elegant white-work one for her wedding bed in 1845. "The whole spread was done with trapunto, a large, stuffed circle in the center, vine and leaves around the border." Sarah was such a perfectionist that she would not let anyone else help her. "Someone picked it up and did a couple of stitches, and she picked them out. She said that was *her* spread."[170]

When Emily Nancy Ballard was married in Liberty Hill, South Carolina, she brought to her new home an even more elaborate bride's quilt. She and her friends had made it of yards and yards of fine white cotton. They had tediously cut out the exotic birds and floral arrangements from expensive, imported chintzes and appliquéd them using the button-hole stitch onto thirty blocks, as well as onto the border around all four sides. Within a chintz wreath of roses and leaves was inscribed "Emily N. Ballard's Quilt 1852"; in another block was the verse "Joined by the lasting ties of love/ and friendship can our hearts forget/ no dearest Em though far removed/ Each thought of thee will still be sweet."[171]

Emily's completed quilt was an elaborate album quilt with her friends' and family's names inscribed on it. Her quilt was similar to those of other brides with means. In rural areas, brides also brought with them quilts to remember their loved ones, but theirs were usually the simpler scrapbag friendship quilts that had become popular with so many brides moving away as soon as they were married. In Mansfield, Connecticut, in 1852, Lucinda Place Howard packed the two bridal friendship quilts she had made for her wedding outfit. Just married, she and Ephraim journeyed to Providence, Rhode Island, where they lived with some of Ephraim's family. Her friendship quilts must have added cheer to her otherwise hard life there. Maybe she remembered the many happy hours with her mother, sisters and neighbors as she had collected cloth from their dresses and shirts and pieced the blocks. Then "she had to make quite a few labels, just a piece of paper pinned onto each block. That way she had kept track of the name that went with it." When Lucinda had posed the question aloud as to how she would do the names, her brother-in-law, William Willis Barrows (with whom she and her widowed mother lived, along with her sister Selina), said he would do them if they wanted him to. He had been teaching school for many years already, even long before he had married Lucinda's sister Selina. There was no question that he had letter-perfect handwriting. On several occasions, then, William Willis sat down with "just an ordinary steel pen" and carefully inscribed Lucinda's blocks, finishing every one by underlining each part of the name with a straightedge. He made no mistakes. There were so many family and friends in the Mansfield area whom she had to include, however, that she had been able to make two complete quilts. So Lucinda had taken a pair of bridal friendship quilts with her that February of 1852.[172]

Ada C. Taylor Dunsmoor also had a friendship quilt when, as a new bride, she went to live with her husband's family in nearby Cavendish, Vermont. Actually, she had begun working on her quilt blocks in 1868, even before her first teachers' examination. She had been fifteen then, planning her future as a schoolmistress. But, four years later, all that was of the past. She was a wife now and had to give up teaching. Many of the blocks of her friendship quilt reminded her of those days; many of the names inscribed on them

HONEYMOON

The word "honeymoon" was used as early as the sixteenth century. The earlier word was "honey-month," but this was considered low class; the proper term among the genteel was "going away." The custom goes back to marriage by capture when the groom had "a hurried flight made necessary by the almost certain wrath of the bride's father." The couple kept out of his way for at least a month. Ethel L. Urlin, A Short History of Marriage *(Detroit: Singing Tree Press, 1969), p. 254.*

Broderie Perse bridal album quilt, by Emily Nancy Ballard, Liberty Hill, South Carolina, 1852, 89 × 108 inches, appliquéd cotton chintzes, with button-hole stitch and ink. *Collection of The Charleston Museum, South Carolina.*

Chimney Sweep, one of a pair by Lucinda Place Howard, Mansfield, Connecticut, made before her February 22, 1852 wedding, 94 × 94 inches, pieced cottons, with ink. *Collection of the author.*

William Willis Barrows, Lucinda's brother-in-law and a schoolteacher, inscribed all the names on the quilt with an ordinary steel pen. At the time Lucinda was piecing her quilt, her uncle on the family homestead next door ran a clothes-making business. Hundreds of yards of the latest, brilliantly printed fabrics were arriving from Hartford, the women of the neighboring farms cutting and sewing them into garments. Thus, there were boxes of scraps of expensive cottons from which Lucinda could have chosen for her creations.

were of fellow schoolmistresses — Corinne Delano, Mary Steel, Mary Marcy, Minnie Labaree, even the present superintendent Walter I. Kendall's wife, Jennie. There were also four persons specially dear to Ada, their blocks inscribed differently from the rest. Lovingly "Mother 1868," "Father," "Walter" and "Grandmother" had been fancifully written and underlined in a flourish. Ada's own block of rose-sprigged calico read simply, "Ada C. Taylor 1872." Her future husband's name was inscribed, within a brown-figured calico, "Alva Dunsmoor."

Even over the international line in the quiet, quaint, rural little hamlet of Abbotts Corner, Quebec, newly married Cynthia Abbott Miner treasured the bridal friendship quilt she had made. It was only of everyday cottons, yet she had pieced the blocks together with an attractive nine-patch setting and tediously quilted every white area with motifs of leaves and flowers, filling in all the areas between with rows and rows of quilting stitches. She had finished the quilt's edge with delicate piping of rose-sprigged calico. Because of the hundreds of hours of work of her hands, Cynthia's quilt was worthy of a special bed and added warmth and color to her farmhouse.

_T_he new bride was so trained and ingrained with the phrase "go to keeping house" that she entered her new home with acceptance and determination to be a good wife. "Home" was now the most important word in her vocabulary. That was her place, and it was up to her to spare no pains to make that place, no matter how crude an abode, comfortable, convenient and attractive.

Now the kitchen was the heart of the new bride's life. She should spend three-quarters of her day there.[173] Over and over she was told that making bread was her most important duty. As Mrs. Cornelius warned in *The Young Housekeeper's Friend* of 1850, "There is no one thing upon which health and comfort in a family so much depend as *bread*. . . . However improbable it may seem, the health of many a professional man is undermined, and his usefulness curtailed, if not sacrificed, because he habitually eats *bad bread*." And the most important and tedious part in making bread was in kneading it. "A half an hour is the least time to be given to kneading a baking of bread. . . . No woman of sense will hesitate in choosing between sour, tough, ill-baked bread, with heaps of wasted pieces, a dyspeptic husband, and sickly children on the one hand, and comfort, economy and health on the other."[174]

Making good bread *dough* was only the beginning. Baking the bread required other skills. Long into the second quarter of the nineteenth century and much later on the frontier, women were still making their bread in ovens built into the bricks of the hearth wall. Instructions in 1850 were vague: "The size and structure of ovens is so different, that no precise rules for heating them can be given. . . . It is easy to find out how many sticks of a given size are necessary for baking articles that require a strong heat; and so for those which are baked with less." And the new bride had to know about different kinds of wood and their heat and burning properties. Most important, she must be able to tell exactly when the oven was the right temperature to put the dough in. There were several methods: one was to "throw in a little flour. If it browns instantly, the oven is too hot, and should stand open three or four minutes. If it browns without burning in the course of half a minute, it will be safe to set in the articles immediately."[174] Perhaps a less wasteful way (for the flour anyway) was to stick one's hand into the oven and be able to hold it there just until the count of twenty, but no more. If she counted correctly, her oven temperature would be just right. No wonder Ellen Spaulding Reed was so proud to have baked "a huge loaf of brown bread" for her new husband, thinking "she had got bread enough to last a day or two." Then how frustrated she must have felt after the hours of work when he "came in at night from ploughing . . . and eat most every mouthful of it."[175]

Although the brick oven was a lot of work, the new stoves had their problems, too. Elisabeth Koren in a Norwegian settlement in Winneshiek County, Iowa, wrote, "I have begun to bake bread. . . . Something went wrong the first time and I was quite disgusted with my new stove, thinking it would not bake properly; but I found a man who taught us how to operate it — it is a new type, it seems. Now all goes well and the other day I ventured to bake white bread. . . . They tasted good but gave Vilhelm a chance to laugh at me because of the remarkable shapes they assumed."[176]

Nannie Tiffany Alderson, a new bride on a crude ranch in Montana, was "a hundred horse-and-buggy miles from a loaf of baker's bread or a paper of pins." There was only "one unpleasant pair" of white women within miles, and her only "guide to housekeeping" was "a cook book and housekeeping manual . . . written by a Southern gentlewoman for Southern gentlewomen," that "didn't contain a single cake recipe that called for fewer than six eggs." As Nannie later said, "Back home in West Virginia I had thought myself quite a housewife. . . . But out here I found that I didn't know, as they say, straight up." Indeed there had been no women to teach her anything once out west; she had learned from "the friendly helpfulness of men"[177] — cowboys on the ranch, as well as her husband.

CARRYING THE BRIDE OVER THE THRESHOLD

The bride was carried over the threshold in ancient Rome because a stumble at that moment was very unlucky. Thresholds were believed to be treacherous places for the gathering of evil spirits.

The new bride in the country also should be skilled in the dairy. The cow was usually her responsibility: milking it, setting the milk, churning it into butter and making cheese. Washing was a major, exhausting task of "fetching and boiling of water, rubbing, scrubbing, rinsing and wringing."[178] After that, the clothes must be starched and laid or hung to dry, often on bushes, the grass, or whatever else would suffice. Then the ironing took great patience and time. With white, cotton pantaloons and as many as ten layers of petticoats fashionable throughout the mid-nineteenth century, she had hours upon hours of ironing for her own undergarments alone. Her dresses of yards and yards of calico also had to be ironed, as well as her husband's linen shirts and pants. Even into the nineteenth century, ironing was a long, hot ordeal, especially in the summertime when two or three irons had to be heated over the oil stove. Ethel Golden suffered sometimes over an hour to do one petticoat. As she explained, "There were yards and yards of cloth in them. You had ruffles, then you would starch them." And even as a young girl her

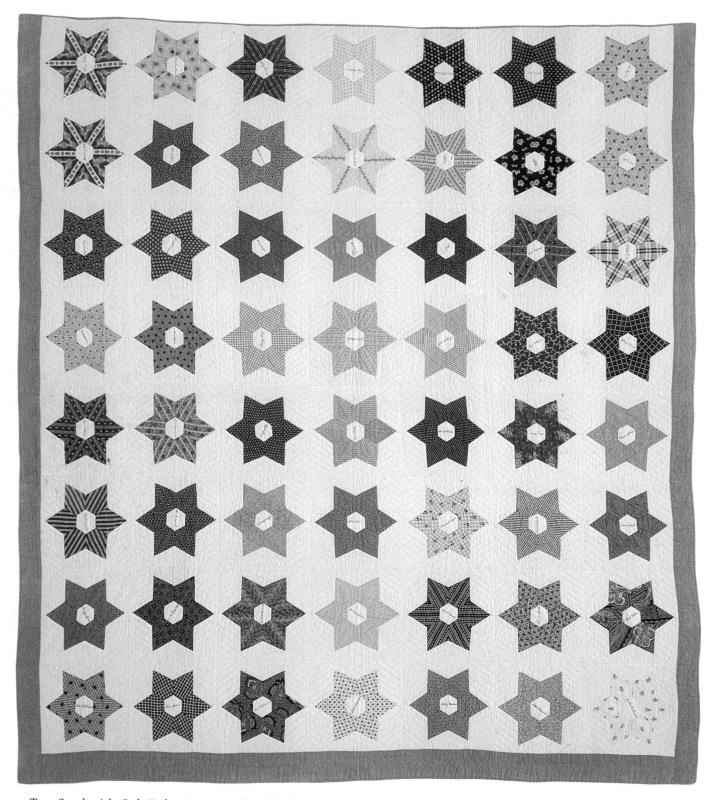

Texas Star, by Ada Cady Taylor Dunsmoor, West Windsor, Vermont, before her marriage, c. 1872, 77½ × 86½ inches, pieced cottons, with ink. *Collection of the author.*
Ada's brother, whose block on the quilt is simply inscribed "Walter," died in a tragic railroad accident only two years after the completion of this quilt.

Unknown quilt pattern, by Cynthia Abbott Miner, Abbotts Corner, Quebec, Canada, before her marriage of December 31, 1863,
81 × 82 inches, pieced cottons, with ink. *Collection of the author.*
Cynthia died in 1904. Her husband gave the quilt to Jane Rockwell Carpenter as a wedding gift the following year. The quilt was found
in one of Jane's trunks in the stone tavern in Alburg, Vermont, in 1984.

mother had warned, "All right, if you're not so careful about your petticoats, you can iron them yourself."[179]

"Hot rolls, plus a vague understanding that petticoats ought to be plain, were [Nannie Tiffany Alderson's] whole equipment for conquering the West." Later on she would bless her "Auntie in Atchison" (West Virginia) for instilling "what little smattering of common sense I had." As Nannie later wrote, "I made all my trousseau myself. Thanks to Auntie I did have sense enough to make my underthings plain according to the standards of the day — so they had some pretense at suitability to the life I was planning to lead." Before she was married in April of 1883, Nannie had never done any washing or ironing; her mother had servants for that. But on a ranch in Montana, she had to learn to do her own work. Then she was grateful that she had made "simpler" petticoats "with just a single deep ruffle tucked solid to hold the starch, and a band of lace whipped to the ruffle," instead of "a mass of lace, and frills upon frills." Her "mother thought them dreadfully plain, but when [Nannie] had to iron them [she] thought them elaborate enough."[180]

With the whale-oil and kerosene lamps, women had another time-consuming job at hand-cleaning the lamp chimneys and refilling them each day. This was Ethel Golden's job as a girl, and she always had "lots of black chimneys to clean" because her father "would never turn down the lamps — he wanted to see where he was going."[181] When a woman's daily work was finished, she mended and patched her husband's ever-deteriorating clothes, then sewed by hand a much-needed pair of pants for him, an apron for herself. She saved her knitting for evenings, when she had less light to work by.

At the day's end many women kept a diary noting the work they had accomplished that day. Maybe they were following advice from *Godey's* to keep a "Housekeeping Journal": "it keeps constantly before you what is to be done," and it helps "place your work out of the way."[182] Ada Taylor Dunsmoor tried to write in her simple little notebook every night. Her diaries were filled with entries denoting work: "Churned 6 1/2 lbs. butter; I hulled some corn for Della; I churned and printed 4 lbs. butter; I've syruped off two bottles caked a little to send to Harold and Della; I canned bal. of fresh meat and smoked bacon; I canned 23 gals. and sugared 25   Sent the sewing I have done for Della also some sugar cakes."[183]

And Ada was continually sewing and knitting on something: "I worked on my night dress; cut out skirt & gingham dress; I began sewing on some night gowns for Geneva and Rebecca; I began a wide strip for my bedspread; Finished 3 night gowns for girlies and a sheet."[183] She had finished knitting her ninth helmet (a tight-fitting hat that covered the ears with a neck band to fit down into the coat, providing necessary protection for Vermont winters), as well as numerous pairs of mittens.

Besides noting her daily accounts, Ada wrote directions for knitting a helmet. She also jotted down directions for "Fly poison to be used on the stable piles,"[183] as well as a long list of the books she had read that year.

Many new brides, like Harriet Fisher Higgins, were alone a major part of their days, removed from everything they knew, in a crowded, dark, one-room log cabin. For Harriet, a new bride of only several months and already pregnant, there were long hours to fill here in this new country high up in the

Green Mountains. To help her endure some of the solitude, some of the separation from her loved ones, she had begun collecting pieced, signed blocks from her family and friends back home for a friendship quilt. Now Harriet looked forward to letters, especially the ones arriving in puffy, over-stuffed envelopes. She gingerly opened each one, excited to read the loving inscription, adding the quilt block to her ever-increasing collection. In order to keep a record of those she had sent blocks, Harriet had numbered each one in the left-hand corner; then, when they were signed and returned, she had an inventory and could know when she had received them all. Unfor-

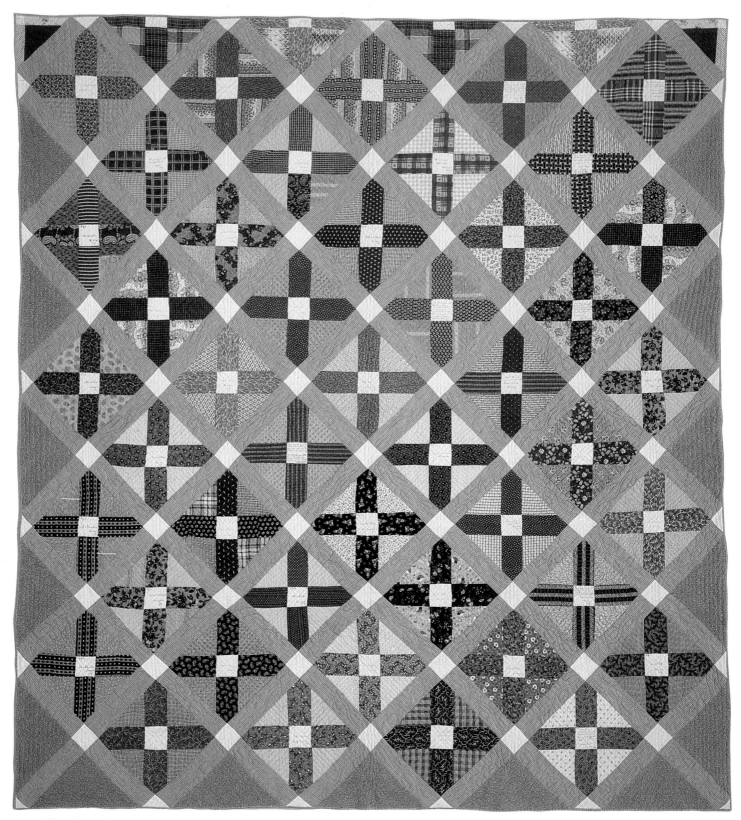

Album Patch, by Harriet Fisher Higgins as a new bride, in her log house in the mountain settlement of West Somerset, Vermont, c. 1851, 85½ × 95½ inches, pieced cottons. *Collection of the author.*

tunately, Number 29 never arrived, as well as several others. She had feared that letters might be lost; after all, there was no post office on this mountain top. Letters had to be addressed to "Somerset" or "West Somerset, Vermont," with an additional direction of "Wilmington," or "Dover, Vt.," along with a note, such as "The postmaster by forwarding this at the first opportunity will oblidge."[184] A letter might take weeks to arrive, having lain on a shelf in one of the country stores in a town down below until her husband or a neighbor would claim it and carry it up the mountain to her.

But Harriet Higgins lived in civilized country compared to Mary Rabb in Spanish Texas in the 1820's, wild Indian territory then. Mary endured days and nights knowing she was completely alone and defenseless while her husband was away. She tried to be brave, putting the dangers out of her mind daily by pounding dry corn kernels into meal for bread or by keeping "her spinning wheel whirring and whistling, sitting outside during the day." Then, when darkness obliterated the land, Mary moved her wheel onto the "earthing" floor by the hearth inside her primitive, rough-hewn log house. She "kept at her spinning, for the roaring of the wheel 'drownded' out the sounds of the Indians 'walking around and hunting mischief.' When Mary became too sleepy to spin . . . she scattered dry corn under her bed and let in the young pigs anxiously waiting under the house. The pigs proved good company, and the crackling of the dry corn was a comforting sound [her "white noise"] as she drifted off to sleep."[185]

For Mary Rabb and Harriet Higgins, there were days when they probably could not get to their spinning or sewing. They were in a new country and had to set aside long periods of time for tasks such as making soap, butter, cheese, maybe even tallow candles — not to mention the round-the-clock care of a new infant. All of a woman's tasks became magnified then, her husband unable or unwilling to help, usually busy elsewhere toiling with an entirely different set of jobs: splitting rail fence, chopping firewood, grubbing, plowing, planting, reaping. His work began at dawn, and many times he was far too exhausted and overworked when he finally came home to have much sympathy for his new wife. Of course, her work had begun even earlier than his, maybe as early as 4 A.M. She had to get the fire going, the water boiling, and a huge breakfast for her beloved so that he would have energy to accomplish his morning's tasks.

There were exceptions to the rule. Ruth Taylor remembers her very kind, loving father getting up at 4 in the morning and letting her mother sleep. While she slept, he carried all the water needed for that day from the well, "quite a little ways"[186] away, as well as prepared his breakfast before his day's work.

But his wife, like other married women across the country, had many children, nine in all, to add to her daily work. Certainly she needed another hour of sleep after having been up during the night nursing the baby and comforting the toddler.

For the typical woman, the first child had been born by the end of the first year of her marriage; she might expect to have a child every two to three years for the next twenty years or so. And she could expect to care for her child without her husband's assistance. Maybe the poem in the January, 1854, issue of *Godey's* sounded all too familiar and provided young mothers a little comfort:

'Twas night, and all day long I'd strove
To soothe my little suffering dove.
Oh, whose beside a mother's love
    Could rightly nurse a baby?
I laid me down to steal some rest,
Its head was pillowed on my breast;
In dreams, my husband's love still blessed
    Me and my darling baby.

But soon its piteous moanings broke
My rest, and from my dreams I woke
To feel its pulse's feverish stroke,
    My little suffering baby!
"And oh, how hot its little head!
Rise quick and get a light, dear Fred!
Something unusual, I'm afraid,
    Is ailing our poor baby."

Slowly he rose, with sullen grace,
The light gleamed on his cloudy face —
"I never knew 'twas a (man's!) place
    Before, to tend a baby!"
My pulses throbbed; a terror crept
Throughout my heart; and, while I wept,
This *noble man* lay down and *slept,*
    And left me with my baby.

Oh, you, light-hearted, beauteous maid,
Whose greatest care's to curl and braid,
Far from life's lessons have you strayed,
    If you ne'er think of babies!
Then learn from me, a matron staid,
For this alone was woman made,
After her sovereign lord's obeyed,
    To nurse and tend the babies.

And Man, thou noblest work of God!
Thou, who canst never see the load
Thy wife sustains through life's rough road,
    With thee and with her babies,
Go kneel upon thy mother's grave
And think — that every life she gave
Made her Death's victim or Life's slave;
    Then love your wife — and babies! [187]

For many settlers, their homes, often only tiny, one-room structures, became impossibly overcrowded and cramped as the children came along. Ideally, the husband would be able to keep one step ahead of his wife and move them all into a commodious home that he had erected nearby on their land. But with all his back-breaking work simply for his family's survival,

Harriet Fisher and Oliver Higgins. *Photographs courtesy of Robert E. and Miriam J. Higgins.*

that was not always the case. Stepping inside Zelotes Gates's log house in April of 1806, one might wonder how he and his family were able to tolerate the situation. As he wrote to his brother, "my children are all active and Easy to Learn   my oldest was Eight years old last December and the youngest one the middle one is a girl   five in all — the youngest very cross he is a roaring now, my Wife has two Sisters Live with us and I have a hired boy which makes ten in a famaly. I have pervision plenty   A good Barn and a poor Noysey Cluttered house and I dont know when I shall get a new one, I have Cider plenty and some apples   my stock & one old mare two Cows   very likely two not so big a pair of twin oxen four years old but small well bilt good to draw handy both ways   Look as much a like as two peas   dark red coler. . . . I intend to come and see you some time or other if I live."[188]

Inside these cramped quarters, the women of the household actually were spinning, weaving and dyeing their wool vivid hues. Somehow, from inside Zelotes's dark cabin, by the light of the hearth or tiny, precious glass window, his wife and her sisters pieced vivid scarlet and green homespun woolen blocks together with black into a striking top and then quilted it with thread they had spun on their wheel. But, from Zelotes's glimpse into his house, there was not room for his wife and her sisters to move about, let alone to quilt. Maybe they quilted as the minister's wife, Elisabeth Koren, did in her

"Little Iowa Parsonage" in 1855: "I lay on the floor a couple of days stitching quilts. I do not have a table large enough.... There, then, I had lain all day long and was very tired, and very happy to be finished."[189]

With childbirth and babies, a woman suffered worries, agonies and grief far beyond any of her daily toil. She chose not even to name her infant for several months, in her need to stay unattached emotionally until she was more certain of its permanence. Over two months after the birth of her sister's little girl, Ellen Spaulding Reed wrote, "I want to know if the baby has got named yet and if she groows [sic] any."[190] Many an unfortunate woman, like young Cynthia Abbott Miner, lost one infant after another. She would work through nine months' pregnancy, bear the agonizing fears and pain of childbirth, then begin nursing her helpless, fragile baby. Cynthia's first child, Edith, actually lived eleven months before dying in January of 1867. Two years later her next

Large family posing in front of their log house, 1912. *Collection of the author.*

child, a little boy, lived only thirty-seven days. He had died so quickly that his grieving parents may have given him the name of Everett posthumously, for the record of his existence on his gravestone. Cruelly, her third child, Grace Lillian, was born one day before what would have been Everett's sixth birthday, and even as Cynthia must have thought about little Everett and his death, Grace Lillian lived but four days longer than he had. Her infant son had died on July 1; Grace Lillian died July 4.

But infancy was not the only critical period in a child's life in the nineteenth century. In fact, there would be no time not to worry. A mother could read or hear the dreaded word of diseases and epidemics in a village or city not too distant. Cholera was killing thousands across the country, as well as throughout the Western world — in New York, Cincinnati, St. Louis, Pittsburgh, even Montreal. In the mid-1800's, the newspapers relayed increasingly alarming statistics; there were 169 cases with 71 deaths in 24 hours in New York alone.[191] One case in the *Vermont Journal* was "peculiarly distressing":

An isolated family in their Sunday "best," with their pets, posing in front of their new commodious home. Remnants of their previous log cabin lie on the ground to the left. Late nineteenth century. *Collection of the author.*

A young man died of the disease and was buried. His widow was sadly afflicted by the event, and expressed a desire to die also. To this end, she is said to have wrapped herself up in the blankets in which her husband had died, and on the day after his burial she was seized with the disease, and next day was a corpse.[192]

There were other diseases, such as diphtheria, typhoid and scarlet fever, at the same time. In Windsor County in Vermont, in 1849 and 1850, scarlet fever killed many children. Mary Mather's friend Caroline Bowen lost her baby boy, Lorenda Tuttle her six-year-old little girl. Then the disease had struck mercilessly at her brother's home at the old homestead: three of Giles Wait's children, Marcus 11 months, Mary Jane 4 years, and Susan 9, all dead and buried within a shockingly short period. And Mary's younger sister Caroline lost her six-year-old daughter, Mary, also. Then, just before Christmas of 1850, Mary's own sixteen-year-old son, William, whom she had come to depend on so since her husband's death a year and a half earlier, died of the disease.

On the plains of the southwest, there were other terrors besides disease. In west Texas, Louisa Ervendberg lost her small son from a rattlesnake bite. The woman of the frontier had to be tough; she had to learn the skills necessary to protect her children. With Annie Oakley as her role model, young Jenny Thompson Higgins, only five feet two and ninety pounds, was a skilled markswoman, able to cut "the top out of a fir tree just like it was a whistle"; she fished for her family's dinner; she killed rattlesnakes, or anything else endangering them. One time she took a hoe and killed a rattlesnake, later telling her children, "The hoe blade was just *wet* with venom." On another occasion Jennie saw something moving in some rocks. She hurled a crowbar at it and "took the hide right off a rabbit."[193]

For the family in newly settled areas in low, damp, marshy land with poor drainage, land in the process of being cleared, the ague (malaria) killed or ruined thousands and thousands of all ages. Like many wives across the country, Harriet Higgins had packed all their belongings and, with a child in arms and one by the hand, she had followed her husband from one remote place to another, from one occupation to another, farming, lumbering, tanning, carpentry. Those were difficult years, especially after they arrived in southern Illinois in a new settlement on the prairie. Her husband had come down with the headache, then the shakes that forced him to bed. Even under a heap of quilts and comfortables, he trembled enough to rattle the bedstead. Oliver had the dreaded ague. It was said that the ague "comes creeping up a fellow's back like a ton of wildcats, goes crawling through his joints like iron spikes." But even though the disease was very serious, many times fatal, so many suffered with it that it was commonly believed, "You should let them run on till they wear themselves out," or die. It was a long time until Harriet knew which would be her husband's fate. Meanwhile Harriet had to carry on the best she could, fearing for her husband's life, worrying that she and the children might also succumb to this common disease of the frontier.[194] But such was the married woman's plight in the west.

Harriet Fisher Higgins was fortunate; her husband not only survived all

LEFT: Ephraim Howard. RIGHT: Lucinda Place Howard with her daughter Mary. *Photographs courtesy of Ethel Golden Nichols, granddaughter.*

the hazards of new settlements and the lumbering business, but he grew disenchanted with the great opportunities of the west and took his wife and family back home to Hinsdale, New Hampshire.

Truly the most devastating loss a woman had to endure was the death of her husband, especially if he were young and they had young children. If he did indeed die young, most likely it was consumption that killed him. That was the disease of young men and women, young husbands and wives. In fact, there were few families that consumption did not touch. Many families lost several of their loved ones to it. In Ascutneyville, Vermont, Mary and Charles Mather's doctor, Dr. Robert Atwood, lost his wife to consumption. Ten years later he would lose his nineteen-year-old daughter to the same disease. And only one year after Mrs. Atwood's death, Mary Mather, draped in yards and yards of heavy dull black silk and densely woven lace, mourned the death of her beloved Charles. Consumption.

In Connecticut, Lucinda Place Howard had heard and suffered enough from that terrifying disease when the doctor diagnosed her son-in-law as consumptive. Her father, Thomas Place, had died of it when she was two years of age. He had been only thirty-one when he had left his wife, Nancy, a widow with three little girls, ages 2, 5 and 9. She had had sufficient time to prepare for his death, having purchased cloth and items for her "Mourning Suit: Bonnet & Veil 3.00, Gown — 2.40, Shoes & Gloves — 2.00, Crape, etc. 4.00," all of it severest, dull black for heavy mourning for the first year.[195] And Thomas, even though "in a declining state of health," typically bequeathed his "dear wife Nancy Place...so long as she remains my widow, and at her decease, or in case of remarriage, the whole of the said estate, goods and chattels...to be equally divided among my children."[196]

Lucinda had been too young to remember her father or his death. All she had of him was an early black silhouette, the side view of him, in her small leather-bound "Album" of tintypes, daguerreotypes and cartes de visite of family and friends. There was another man in the album, a picture of a handsome man, middle-age, bearded. He too had died of consumption. Only 59. Yes, Lucinda had grieved as her own mother had grieved, for she too had had to endure her dear husband's gradual, hideous wasting away, that unforgettable cough. And she would never forget her pain when their daughter, Mary, only thirteen, had pleaded to kiss her father goodnight, and she and Ephraim had had to forbid that last farewell. After all that, it must have seemed a miracle, truly an answer to their prayers, when Mary's own husband, Morris, had recovered. Finally doctors were having success in their treatments.

But, in the nineteenth century, there had been no explanation as to how one got the disease. There were all kinds of advertised cures, yet death seemed always inevitable. Out of desperation, the superstition grew "that a vine or root of some kind grew from coffin to coffin, of those of one family, who died of consumption, and were buried side by side; and when the growing vine had reached the coffin of the last one buried, another one of the family would die, the only way to destroy the influence or effect, was to break the vine; take up the body of the last one buried and burn the vitals, which would be an effectual remedy." Accordingly, after six or seven in his family had died, and then his daughter also seemed consumptive, one man in Dummerston, Vermont, dug up his most recently deceased loved one, immediately burned the vitals; and his daughter "it is affirmed, got well and lived many years."[197]

For many women whose husbands and children had miraculously escaped disease, there were other horrors. With the Industrial Age there were dangerous occupations and monstrous machinery. For Ada Taylor Dunsmoor, the date of December 2, 1874, was slashed and stabbed into her very soul, for it had been the time of nightmarish horror for her and her family. The first day of December had been a brisk, wintry day. Fewer and fewer wagons were to be seen as most everyone had retired them for their winter sleighs and sleds. Down at the depot, melted snow had frozen over, making her husband's and brother Walter's work treacherous. Family and neighbors later read that Walter "was out switching, and slipped on the ice and fell across the track. Just then, freight train No. 20 passed along and cut off both his legs above the knee."[198] This unforeseen tragedy had enshrouded the stone house for-

Walter Taylor's gravestone, in the cellar of the old stone house in West Windsor, Vermont.
The family shared overwhelming grief, as well as a dilemma: where could they bury Walter? It was winter and the ground was impenetrable, lying under many inches of snow and ice.

ever, marring the lives of those inside.

Whether directly or indirectly, the brutality of war touched almost every nineteenth-century woman. There were many: Indian attacks and battles on the frontier, the War of 1812, the Alamo, the Mexican War, the Spanish-American War and the most brutal war of the century, the War between the States. With Fort Sumter fired upon on April 12, 1861, women put aside their flowered calicoes for new dresses, the white cotton for their little girls' "panteletts"; instead, they sewed for the soldiers, shirts for boys like their own to wear into battle, woven reticules soldiers would carry with them. Women also met at town halls and churches "to ravel lint from squares of cloth for dressings for the wounded soldiers."[199] Every day there was talk of war. Daily, boys were leaving from the north, from the south, headed to meet one another in bloody battle. Every night young girls, sweethearts, wives and mothers alike picked up their pens and wrote into their diaries of "this terrible War."[200] In West Windsor, Vermont, Mary Mather Steel's son Fred and her sister's boy Charles Dake were among the forty-two soldiers of the West Windsor Guards who left, fife and drum cheering them on, that somber day of September 25, 1862, headed for Virginia. Mary and her sister waited and prayed. Every day the news grew more frightening. In nearby Weathersfield, "Justice Dartt, Frank Dartt, and John Bennett have been taken prisoners by the rebels."[201] "Mr. Marcy's folks received a letter last night containing the dreaded news of Oliver's death."[202] Mary Mather Steel's neighbors, the Lamsons, Gateses and Burnhams, all grieved over the deaths of their sons. In Weathersfield, even fifteen-year-old Marietta Rice penned into her diary, "O! the dreadful war, when will it ever end."[203] Four of Mary Hammond's boys from down the road were in Virginia. Thanksgiving Day had been grim, with many chairs around those long farm tables empty. Mary Hammond had baked only one "chicken for Supper & had Enough left for Dinner."[204]

For many, the Civil War had greedily taken their sons, sending them home wounded or maimed, killing thousands and thousands more from disease and injury. Mary Mather Steel and Mary Hammond were both very thankful: their boys had returned home healthy.

But for mothers whose children had survived, there were always the advertisements, the propaganda, the overly enthusiastic letters from a relative or former neighbor to pack up, bring as much money as they could get together and invest in the west. There were those mothers that would hug their ambitious sons goodbye, bound for some new government lands, never to see or even to hear from them again. Such was the plight of Harriet Fisher Higgins. Her son Alfred had always been very independent and strong-minded. He was not unlike his father in his determination to succeed, but in Hinsdale, New Hampshire, he had to work long, grueling hours within a labyrinth of brick walls of the woolen mill. There was no hope of his ever getting ahead, having a wife and two little children to support. He had begun considering going west. His dad's brother Uncle Newman and family were out in Illinois, but Alfred would have to go much further to homestead in the 1880's. Letters, pamphlets and promoters proclaimed "the money-making potential that awaited the 'opportunist'" in Colorado. One widely circulated

The Wait homestead, West Windsor, Vermont, birthplace and girlhood home of Mary Wait Mather Steel. *Photograph courtesy of the West Windsor Historical Society, Brownsville, Vermont.*
Mary's maternal grandfather, Captain Samuel Savage, bought the original fifty-acre lot of land in 1774 when it had been part of Cumberland County, New York. Adding land in 1788 and 1789, he built his first house of logs. His daughter Prudence married Allen Wait in 1800, and they went to housekeeping with the Savages. Mary was born in a log house that her father had built on the hill. In 1825, when Mary was eleven, 112 yoke of oxen moved that log house down near the road. The homestead stayed in the Wait family throughout Mary's lifetime, belonging to her brother Giles Wait and then to her nephew Galon C. Wait.

Alfred Higgins as a young boy. *Photograph courtesy of grandson Robert E. and Miriam J. Higgins.*

pamphlet stated, "Those who are restless in their old homes, and who seek to better their condition, will find greater advantages in Colorado than any-where else in the west. . . . The *poor* should come to Colorado, because here they can by industry and frugality better their condition. . . . The *young* should come here to get an early start on the road to wealth."[205]

Alfred was already in his thirties. He was a skilled carpenter having to work in a woolen mill, where he would most likely work the rest of his life — if he stayed in New England.

It was in the mid-1880's that Harriet had tearfully said good-bye to her son, not knowing when she might see him again. He and his wife Cora and the little ones left on the train headed for Denver, over 2,000 miles away in the new state of Colorado. Years had passed, years of agonizing waiting for Harriet. Was her son even alive? She had no way of knowing. Nor could

Harriet have imagined how difficult life was in Colorado for Alfred. Shortly after arriving there, he and Cora had been through a devastating divorce. Cora had remained in Denver working as a servant in order to support herself.[206] The children were elsewhere.

At this time it was easier for Alfred or Cora to secure a divorce in Colorado than it would have been in the east. The actual grounds for divorce were not unlike those of the eastern states (impotency, bigamy, adultery, desertion, extreme or repeated acts of cruelty, failure of husband to provide for his family, habitual drunkenness, and conviction of felony), but the term of residency was not so rigid in the west. Unless "upon grounds of adultery or extreme cruelty"[207] committed within the state, Colorado required only one year of residency. The greatest deterrent and difficulty in a divorce in some states, such as New York and South Dakota, was that the guilty party could not remarry during the lifetime of the innocent party. Fortunately for Alfred, this was not the case in Colorado, so in April of 1890 he had married Jenny Florence Thompson of Denver. Alfred was 39, Jenny only 15. The next years they had homesteaded, Jenny having a child every year and a half or so. For many years Alfred was too poor to allow his mother to come see him. He had too much pride for that. Maybe someday when they had things nicer.... Sadly, the day was never to come. By the time Alfred was finally doing well as a carpenter, having moved to Boise, Idaho, Harriet's strength and health were failing, her feet and legs swelling up to her knees so that it was difficult for her even to see her son Orson and his family down near the river at the Point only several miles away. Letters were all she could hope for. She was resigned to that as she wrote to one of Alfred's daughters, "If I was a few years yonger and had money I would call on you all for I would like to see you so much but hear I am   I cannot go off of the hill so hear I must be."[208]

Since Harriet could not go in person, she wanted to send something of herself to Alfred and Jenny's daughters, something tangible they would have to remember her by, to tell them she loved them. Soon three patchwork tops hand-pieced by Grandmother Harriet Fisher Higgins arrived in Boise, Idaho. It had been the natural thing for Harriet to make quilt tops to connect the distance between her family. Her own friendship quilt had done that for her so many years earlier. Even though Lucy, Gladys and Marguerite Higgins were never to meet their grandmother in person, the warmth of her love had touched them and would remain with them always. Those simple, somber-colored patchwork tops would be the connecting pieces of their lives.

SUPERSTITIONS

An American bride walks alongside her husband on the wedding day. Anyone walking in between them could mean a separation or parting in their marriage. In fact, there must be no separation of the bride and groom on the way to the wedding.

A sharp or pointed object given as a wedding gift was forbidden: it would sever the romance.

A pine cone under the pillow secures a husband's fidelity.

Happy the bride the sun shines on.

A solar eclipse on the wedding day means bad fortune ahead.

Wedding snow is a fortunate occurrence meaning a "rain of riches."

Rain means there will be tears ahead.

*A*cross rural America, there were occasional breaks in the married woman's toil, from her hardships and sorrows. As Marion Dana Hastings remembered, "There were so many things that were fun. It seems people had more time then than we do now." Women looked forward to the times in the spring and the fall when the country peddler would make his way along the dirt roads to their front doors. There were several peddlers that usually came: the pack peddler had his satchel stuffed full of notions, pins, thread, needles, sewing materials, spectacles, pocket knives, straight razors, jew's harps, combs and shoelaces. The one with a wagon would have all kinds of household things, a couple of bundles of brooms finishing off the back of the wagon. Then there was the tin peddler, who rattled and clanged over the rutted roads with tinware of every kind: tin cups and dippers, pie pans, teakettles, dishpans, wash basins, pails of all sizes for carrying milk from the barn or water from the well. His shiny items were popular items of necessity, as well as good gifts for a new bride. And the farm wife did not need money; he took her rags in exchange for some tin household articles. Marion Dana Hastings remembers, "It was always a treat [for the peddler to come] because we'd never see those kinds of things. . . . We always bought something."[209]

One of the peddlers familiar around West Windsor, Vermont, was "Apodeldoc Edson," who sold "essences and extracts. He came from [nearby] Felchville and was a frequent caller in the neighborhood. He was a big, fat man who drove a small bony horse hitched to a wagon which had two chests (looked like trunks) one in front and he sat on the one in back. The wagon had 4 posts which supported a top, but <u>no fringe</u>! He sold all kinds of home remedies but his featured article was 'Apodeldoc.' This he compounded himself. It was a white liquid thick and soapy looking. On the orange label were listed all the exlirior [sic] ailments that man or woman might fall heir to — and it was guaranteed to cure them all! It was advisable to read the label before you removed the rubber stopper because when you did, the ammonia fumes immediately obliterated your vision and copious tears fell."[210] There was a jingle about the peddler:

> Apodeldoc Edson —
> He sells med-c'en!
> He also sells bay rum,
> Better give his o'l hoss some!

"With every change of the season there were things that were fun."[211] In the fall there were corn huskings. "The field corn was cured in the shock out in the fields" and "carted into the barn. Then some evening the farmer would invite all his friends and neighbors to come to a husking bee. As the corn was husked they would throw it into a large pile in the middle of the barn floor. When a gentleman found a red ear then the fun began. He took the ear of corn to the girl of his choice and kissed her — that is if he was able to catch her. At one husking the girl ran into the house and upstairs and he lost both the girl and the kiss."[212]

There were also "apple paring evenings," when the neighbor women would

Barn raising for Galon C. Wait, Mary Mather Steel's nephew, at the Wait homestead in West Windsor, Vermont, 1881. *Photograph courtesy of the West Windsor Historical Society, Brownsville, Vermont.*

get together and pare and slice apples, then spread them out "on racks hung over the kitchen stove to dry. They would stir it up occasionally. Then store it in bags. When they wanted apple pies (after the fresh fruit was gone) they would soak the dried apples in water over night and then make their pies." But those pies were not so popular as the fresh ones. As the old jingle went, "Tread on my corns or tell me lies/ But don't pass me dried apple pies."[212]

Of course, quilting bees were always a highpoint in a married woman's life. She could participate in those in spite of her husband's being too busy in the fields to accompany her. Only six weeks in Burke, Wisconsin, Ellen Spaulding Reed had "not been a visiting yet nor had company but once," but she had quilted on several occasions: "Mrs Cady came and spent one afternoon and I have been and helped her quilt two afternoons   she had a great quilting   there was a lot of the neighbors there and some of them spoke to me and some went home without as much as saying why do you so. . . . I expect they were affraid they should get bit."[213] No matter if some ladies did not talk to her; Ellen entered her tiny, crude log house that evening with a smile on her face, excited and inspired with fresh conversation and gossip to entertain her husband. For Ellen, a new bride in the west, the quilting restored her with hope of brighter days in the future.

Barn raisings were also festive occasions for men, women and children alike. In 1881, there was a huge barn raising in West Windsor, Vermont. Most everyone for miles around had been there to help Mary Mather Steel's nephew Galon C. Wait erect his enormous barn on the old Giles Wait farm. The men actually raised the barn, but the women were the ones to make the feast for later that day with tables and tables of meats, vegetables, relishes, breads, donuts, cakes and pies.

One of the most important celebrations in the countryside was a wedding anniversary. There were "The Five Weddings," as *Godey's* described:

Wooden, Tin, Silver, and Golden Weddings mark the fifth, tenth, twenty-fifth, and fiftieth anniversaries of matrimony. There is, we believe, a Glass Wedding also, but that is an innovation, for nothing as brittle as glass should be used commemorative of the nuptial tie. A wooden wedding can be a very tasteful affair. Lately a wooden wedding was given by a happy five years' wife, in which the rooms were ornamented with festoons of shavings, pictures decorated with shavings, mottoes inscribed on the walls with shavings, the effect of which was exquisitely tasteful and unique. The presents of course were wooden, and in such variety and character — from a knot chopping-bowl to an elaborately carved paper-cutter, from a rolling-pin to an exquisitely finished parlor bracket — as to excite one's special wonder that so many useful and ornamental things can be made from wood.[214]

Ada and Alva Dunsmoor's friends George and Clarissa Spear, married ten years, invited a "vast number" of friends to their large, two-story frame house in Hartland, Vermont, to celebrate "with a tin wedding." As the *Vermont Journal* stated, "Mr. Spear . . . did everything in his power to make everybody pleased, and he succeeded, as it was daybreak before the company had all departed." There was music and dancing and even "Squire Marcy and wife . . . shook 'the light fantastic toe' as lively as some of the youngest."[215]

Of course, the fiftieth anniversary was the most special and meaningful. For Ada Taylor Dunsmoor in West Windsor, her marriage to Alva had truly been one of the most devoted love and tender companionship. They had always been very close, Ada helping Alva as superintendent of schools, even though as a married woman she was not allowed to teach herself. Then he had been supportive of her after the children were raised, when she had run the innovative "school bus," driving her wagon through the winding back roads of the hamlet to outlying farmhouses, picking up the children for school, returning them in the late afternoons no matter the extremes of weather.[216] Alva and Ada had truly shared fifty years of great joys and terrible, terrible sorrow. Their fiftieth anniversary was deservedly a cause for a great celebration in the old stone house.

The celebration was planned for Tuesday, September 18, 1923, the date of their fiftieth wedding anniversary. With the day only one week away, Ada was very busy: she "ironed, cleaned dish cup board, canned beets . . . cleaned parlor; . . . canned corn." As the day grew nearer, Ada had more and more help and also more work: friends and family were arriving from out of town, even cousins Dennis and Becky from Iowa; neighbors were coming over to help and to visit. Alva had his hands full, too, trying to carry on his farm, as well as to entertain. The rooms of the stone house were trimmed with bright crepe paper and other decorations. Letters of congratulations arrived daily; neighbors came calling. The Cabots brought "a china fruit set for a wedding present." Belle was making "pies etc, for the dinner." The night of the 18th, after all the celebrating was over, after all the laughter and congratulations, Ada did not fail to spend a few quiet moments with her diary: "50th wedding

---

LEFT TO RIGHT: Harold Dunsmoor, Ada Dunsmoor, Daisy Demke, Al Demke, Alva Dunsmoor, Martha Demke Dunsmoor, in front of the Dunsmoor home, 1914. *Photograph courtesy of John A. Dunsmoor, grandson of Ada and Alva.*

Ada and Alva Dunsmoor on their porch. *Photograph courtesy of John A. Dunsmoor, their grandson.*

anniversary — Had a family reunion at dinner — 36 were here in P.M. others called — We had a very pleasant time and some nice presents."[217]

Her Golden wedding — that was her celebration, her one moment of commemoration. For couples like Ada Taylor and Alva Dunsmoor, those fifty years together were a tribute to marriage, to *their* marriage, a true sharing and understanding, being partners despite life's precipices and vales. They loved and cherished each other deeply, as only daily devotion to one another over many, many years could achieve.

In the countryside of Vermont in 1927, a widower mourned the loss of his wife. Alva Dunsmoor was so deeply devoted to his Ada that he could not stay in the old stone house for very long after her death. That land had been in the Taylor family for over a century; the house itself bore the stone over the front door, "P.T. 1848," that was put there by her grandfather. And inside the house was so much of Ada: everywhere Alva looked he saw his beloved wife's touch: in her parlor with her Estey organ, in the early winter kitchen of her youth with its fireplace and brick oven, in her kitchen with the iron sink she had greased every day, in her pantry still stocked from the loving work of her hands, her glider on the porch screened in by the gorgeous blue clematis once planted by Ada's hands.

His grief over her death was his greatest tribute to marriage and his beloved wife. After all those years, well over half a century, Ada's goodness filled his heart with overwhelming love, overwhelming grief. "She had gone without the least struggle or a movement — the most peaceful passing I ever knew," Alva wrote. "I have lain awake many nights thinking of the terrible ending that [I] had expected to see if I outlived her but guess the Almighty thought she was too good to have such an ending."[218]

Many, many years had passed since Alva stood holding Ada's hand, promising to love and to cherish her for as long as they both should live. They had been young then, naïve and unknowing of the difficult road that lay ahead. But truly they had fulfilled that promise. They had shared an inseparable bond, a kindred spirit. They had reached into one another's soul and known the ultimate reward of marriage. Even death would not, *could not* separate them: they would ever be part of one another.

*M*en received notice in the newspapers for their military achievements, their early settlement of towns, their wealth and accomplishments. Married women's lives were noted by men in those same papers for their remarkable progeny and longevity. Those were the only memorial, lasting, public tributes to the married woman, the only way she might have a short paragraph about her life as well as a notice of her death.

Across America there were many remarkable women like Elizabeth Honoria Frances Lambe, who died in September of 1839, aged 110 years, 4 months. "She was eight times married, had numerous generations, 260 of whom are now alive, and died an example of true piety."[219] And in Enfield, Connecticut, March 5, 1831, appeared the obituary of "Priscilla, widow of Abraham Johnson, 102 years and 6 mo. She lived in that town for 39 years, and never had any sickness that required a doctor; her descendants are 9 children, 75 grand children, 182 great grand children, and of the 4th generation 6, and of the 5th generation 1."[220]

But then what greater, more encompassing tribute could be made of her married life than that — that she suffered the pangs of labor *many* times, the years of sleepless nights nursing infants and comforting sick little ones, that she clothed them and fed them by the work and ingenuity of her hands alone, that she trained them all to go out into the world, her young women to make homes for their husbands, her young men to venture to new government lands, to found towns, to build the west. Her great numbers of offspring would touch every corner of the country. Her constant, steadfast, day-to-day persistence and devotion would go with them, a part of all that they were and a part of all they ever would be.

With love she would be remembered, for the love she herself had imparted could *never* be forgotten.

REFERENCES

1. Katie Reed McWilliams to Stedman Spaulding, Lathrop, Missouri, March 24, 1884. Courtesy of Barbara Chiolino.

2. Ellen Spaulding Reed to Stedman and Arterista Spaulding, continuation of letter begun by J. Willard Reed, Burke, Wisconsin, February 3, 1856.

3. Penelope Franklin, ed., *Private Pages: Diaries of American Women 1830s – 1970s* (New York: Ballantine Books, 1986), pp. 317 – 318.

4. Diary of Lavina Thomas Gates, entry of July 20, 1864. Collection of San Joaquin County Historical Museum, Stockton, California.

5. Nancy Barnard Batchelder, "Growing Up in Peru (1815 – 1840)," *Vermont Quarterly: A Magazine of History*, XXI, 5.

6. "Origin of the Term Spinsters," *Vermont Journal*, VI, April 19, 1850.

7. [By a Grandmother], *Bessie; or, Reminiscences of a Daughter of a New England Clergyman of the Eighteenth Century* (New Haven: J. H. Benham, 1861), pp. 34, 35, 200.

8. *Bessie*, pp. 199, 213.

9. Mary Caroline Crawford, *Social Life in Old New England* (New York: Grosset & Dunlap, 1914), p. 209.

10. Oscar Theodore Barck, Jr. and Hugh Talmage Lefler, *Colonial America* (New York: The Macmillan Company, 1958), p. 446. Words quoted are those of William Byrd II.

11. Arthur W. Calhoun, *A Social History of The American Family From Colonial Times to the Present* (New York: Barnes & Noble, Inc., 1945), I, 69.

12. Batchelder, p. 9.

13. Nancy Woloch, *Women and the American Experience* (New York: Alfred A. Knopf, 1984), p. 20.

14. Calhoun, I, 68.

15. Ellen Spaulding Reed to Stedman and Arterista Spaulding, continuation of letter begun by J. Willard Reed, March 17 – 19, 1856. Courtesy of Barbara Chiolino.

16. Ellen Spaulding Reed to Stedman and Arterista Spaulding, October 21, 1855, Burke, Wisconsin. Courtesy of Barbara Chiolino.

17. "Search for Wives," *Vermont Journal*, IV, no. 2, July 2, 1847, p. 1.

18. "Young Ladies, Beat This if You Can," *Vermont Journal*, VI, no. 34, February 8, 1850.

19. Rebecca M. Garland to Linda Otto Lipsett, September 14, 1988, Portland, Maine.

20. "Female Character," *The Happy Home and Parlor Magazine*, VI (1857), 67.

21. Lydia Maria Child, *The American Frugal Housewife* (Boston: Carter, Hendee, and Co., 1833), pp. 111, 92.

22. From an advertisement in *Godey's* in January, 1854, "the 'Book' always has a prominent place on the centre-table, and probably remains there until the volume is completed for binding.... Every subscriber's copy is, no doubt, read by at least twenty persons — thus giving to the advertisers in the Lady's Book a larger circulation for their advertisements than can be given by any publication in the United States." *Godey's Lady's Book and Magazine*, XLVIII, January 1854, p. 94.

23. *Godey's Lady's Book and Magazine*, LXXIV, May 1867, p. 477.

24. "Advice to Unmarried Ladies," *Vermont Journal*, VI, July 20, 1849.

25. Definition of "slops," given by Delma Cothran Thames, editor of *A Pinch of This and a Handful of That* (Austin, Texas: Eakin Press, 1988): "a conglomeration of mess, usually pretty liquid for the hogs." Telephone conversation, February 1989.

26. Thames, p. 64.

27. *Godey's Lady's Book and Magazine*, LXXV, July 1867, p. 87.

28. June Sprigg, *Domestick Beings* (New York: Alfred A. Knopf, 1984), p. 17.

29. Sprigg, p. 22.

30. Eliza Southgate Browne, *A Girl's Life Eighty Years Ago* (New York, 1887), letter to Moses Porter, 1801. Quoted in Old Sturbridge Village resource packet "Life Cycle: Courtship and Marriage" (Sturbridge, Mass.: Old Sturbridge Village Museum Education Department, 1978).

31. Franklin, pp. 306 – 307.

32. Justin G. Turner and Linda Levitt Turner, *Mary Todd Lincoln* (New York: Alfred A. Knopf, 1972), p. 21.

33. "Old Maids," *Vermont Quarterly*, XLIII, p. 90. (Originally from the *Green Mountain Gem*, V [1847], Bradford, Vermont.)

34. *Godey's Lady's Book*, LII, February 1856, p. 187.

35. *Godey's Lady's Book*, LII, February 1856, p. 159.

36. *Godey's Magazine and Lady's Book*, XXIX, August 1844, p. 84.

37. Child, p. 92.

38. Browne, *loc. cit.*

39. Letter of recollections of David M. Bell, Alburg, Vermont, November 2, 1988.

40. Henry Reed Stiles, *Bundling: Its Origin, Progress and Decline in America* (New York: Book Collectors Association, Inc., 1869. Republished Detroit: Gale Research Company, 1973), p. 113.

41. Margaret Baker, *Wedding Customs and Folklore* (Totowa, New Jersey: Rowman and Littlefield, 1977), p. 23.

42. Stiles, pp. 85 – 87.

43. Baker, p. 26.

44. "Those early Americans had a good time, too," *the Chronicle* (Willimantic, Conn.), CVI, August 30, 1988, p. 6.

45. Jessica Nicoll, "A Legacy Recognized," *Old Sturbridge Visitor*, XXVIII, no. 1, p. 4.

46. Interview with Ethel Golden Nichols, South Windham, Connecticut, July 23, 1988. Lucinda Place Howard lived with Ethel's family until her death in 1910. Ethel spent many hours with her grandmother, and she vividly remembers many of their conversations, reaching back 150 years to Lucinda's girlhood in the 1830's.

47. Telephone conversation with ninety-year-old Marion Dana Hastings, West Windsor, Vermont, November 18, 1987.

48. Harriet and Fred Rochlin, *Pioneer Jews: A New Life in the Far West* (Boston: Houghton Mifflin Company, 1984), p. 90.

49. Ell B. Rockwell to Lucy Ann McElroy, October 3, 1855, Champlain, Vermont. Courtesy of Robert McHugh; now in Special Collections, Bailey/Howe Library, University of Vermont, Burlington.

50. From poem written in Ell B. Rockwell's hand to Lucy Ann McElroy during their courtship. Courtesy of Robert McHugh; now in Special Collections, Bailey/Howe Library, University of Vermont, Burlington.

51. Carl Sandburg, *The Prairie Years and The War Years* (New York: Harcourt, Brace & World, Inc., 1954), p. 57. Abraham Lincoln to Mary Owens, Springfield, Illinois, May 7, 1837.

52. Ruth Painter Randall, *Mary Lincoln: Biography of a Marriage* (Boston: Little, Brown and Company, 1953), p. 70.

53. Mary never called her husband "Abraham"; she always called him "Mr. Lincoln" or "Father." "No proper wife of that era was so disrespectful as to call her husband by his first name." Ruth Painter Randall, p. 75.

54. Jacob R. Marcus, *The American Jewish Woman: A Documentary History* (New York: KTAV Publishing House, Inc., 1981), p. 241.

55. "Language of the Handkerchief," part of an advertising campaign by Desmond & Company, c. 1871, postcard printed by the Vermont Historical Society, Montpelier, Vermont.

56. Sue Gibson Byrd and Mary Frances Drake, "Andrew Johnson, The Tailor President," *Dress*, XI (1985), 79.

57. Rochlin, p. 83.

58. David Crockett, *A Narrative of The Life of David Crockett of the State of Tennessee* (Knoxville: The University of Tennessee Press, 1973), p. 65.

59. William J. Brown, *Autobiography of William J. Brown* (Freeport, New York: Books for Libraries Press, 1971), p. 155. Quoted in "Life Cycle." The name of Brown's intended is not included in the excerpts.

60. Priscilla Robertson, *Lewis Farm: A New England Saga* (Norwood, Mass.: The Plimpton Press, 1950), p. 36. There was the option of purchasing a marriage license, but that was expensive and used only by the wealthy. Wedding banns were much more common. Their purpose was to prevent clandestine marriages, especially bigamous marriages. In the many instances when the bride's or groom's background was unknown, three weeks was thought to be adequate time for negative information to come to light.

61. L. H. Butterfield, ed., *Diary and Autobiography of John Adams* (New York: Atheneum, 1964), I, 188.

62. From the diary of Elizabeth Ann Jennison, in "Life Cycle."

63. From original Banns of Marriage of Lucinda Place and Ephraim Howard, Mansfield, Connecticut. Courtesy of Ethel Golden Nichols, granddaughter.

64. Robert W. Steele and Mary Davies Steele, *Early Dayton* (Dayton, Ohio: U.B. Publishing House, 1896), p. 62.

65. Maud Wilder Goodwin, *Dolly Madison* (New York: Charles Scribner's Sons, 1896), pp. 31, 32.

66. *Vermont Journal*, VI, no. 5, July 20, 1849.

67. William S. Rossiter, ed., *Days and Ways in Old Boston* (Boston: R. H. Stearns and Company, 1915), pp. 65, 66.

68. Calhoun, II, 13.

69. Steele, p. 62.

70. Calhoun, II, 13.

71. Betty J. Mills, *Calico Chronicle: Texas Women and Their Fashions 1830–1910* (Lubbock: Texas Tech Press, 1985), p. 159.

72. Calhoun, II, 15.

73. "The Old-Fashioned Courtship," *New York World*, from the scrapbook of Laura Kendall Hoadley, South Woodstock, Vermont, c. 1889. Collection of the Norman Williams Public Library, Woodstock, Vermont.

74. Telephone conversation with Yoshiye Sato Tsuboi, daughter of Oriyo Shiote Sato, Los Angeles, March 29, 1989.

75. Telephone conversation with Masaye Sato Kato, daughter of Oriyo Shiote Sato, Los Angeles, March 29, 1989.

76. Tsuboi conversation.

77. Kato conversation.

78. Calhoun, I, 316.

79. *Godey's Magazine and Lady's Book*, XXIX, August 1844, pp. 86–87.

80. Fred Lockley, *The Lockley Files: Conversations with Pioneer Women*, ed. Mike Helm (Eugene, Oregon: Rainy Day Press, 1981), pp. 64–65.

81. Lockley, p. 10.

82. Lockley, pp. 7, 11.

83. John Carver, *Sketches of New England* (New York, 1842), pp. 271–272.

84. Albert Prescott Paine, ed., *History of Samuel Paine, Jr. and his wife Pamela (Chase) Paine of Randolph, Vt. and their Ancestors and Descendants* (Randolph Center, Vermont: privately printed, 1923), p. 47.

85. Alice Morse Earle, *Two Centuries of Costume in America* (New York: The Macmillan Company, 1903), II, 636–637.

86. Goodwin, p. 32.

87. Abby Maria Hemenway, ed., "The Towns of Windham County," *Vermont Historical Gazetteer* (Brandon, Vt.: Mrs. Carrie E. H. Page, 1891), V, 18.

88. Mary Caroline Crawford, p. 220.

89. "A Singular Marriage Ceremony," *The New England Historical & Genealogical Register* (Boston: New England Historic-Genealogical Society, 1867), XXI, 284.

90. Mary Caroline Crawford, p. 221.

91. Mary Caroline Crawford, p. 220.

92. Hemenway, V, 18.

93. Mary Caroline Crawford, p. 220.

94. "Marriage of a Widow," *The New-England Historical and Genealogical Register* (1883), XXXVII, 407. Because of the delicate subject matter, the surnames were omitted in this Victorian publication.

95. David Lufkin Mansfield, *The History of the Town of Dummerston* (Ludlow, Vt: Miss A. M. Hemenway, 1884), p. 26.

96. Robertson, p. 15.

97. *Bessie*, pp. 215–217.

98. Ann Fears Crawford and Crystal Sasse Ragsdale, *Women in Texas: Their Lives, Their Experiences, Their Accomplishments* (Burnet, Texas: Eakin Press, 1982), pp. 16–18.

99. Conversation with Ethel Golden Nichols, South Windham, Connecticut, October 1987.

100. *Bessie*, pp. 201–202.

101. Ralph Tennal, *History of Nemaha County, Kansas* (Lawrence: Standard Publishing Co., 1916), p. 135.

102. Conversation with Barbara Chiolino, Rutland, Vermont, August 1988.

103. Kay Staniland and Santini M. Levey, "Queen Victoria's Wedding Dress and Lace," *Costume: The Journal of the Costume Society* (England), XVII, 5.

104. Staniland, pp. 5–6.

105. [Anonymous], *The Art of Good Behavior* (New York: C. P. Huestis, 1848), pp. 47–48.

106. Harriet Connor Brown, *Grandmother Brown's Hundred Years 1827–1927* (Boston: Little, Brown and Company, 1930), p. 78.

107. "Late News from California," *Vermont Journal*, V, June 8, 1849.

108. Shane Adler, "A Diary and a Dress," *Dress*, V, 83, 88.

109. From the Material Culture Collections, The Charleston Museum, South Carolina.

110. Eliza Ripley, *Social Life in Old New Orleans* (New York: Arno Press, 1975), pp. 266–268. Originally published in 1912.

111. Betty Parham, "Dixie Memories," *The Atlanta Journal and Constitution,* June 9, 1985, p. 4H.

112. Mills, pp. 119–120.

113. David Holman and Billie Persons, *Buckskin and Homespun: Frontier Texas Clothing* (Austin: The Wind River Press, 1979), p. 12.

114. Mills, p. 104.

115. Mills, p. 91.

116. Telephone interview with 95-year-old Ruth Taylor, Garden City, Kansas, July 1988.

117. *Godey's Lady's Book and Magazine,* CXIII, October 1886, p. 378.

118. "A Happy Occasion," *The Bennington* (Vermont) *Banner,* February 21, 1884.

119. Letter by Maud Dinsmore, *Richford Gazette,* Richford, Vermont, April 26, 1883. Reprint courtesy of Barbara Chiolino.

120. "Jane's sister Josie always referred to her as 'Lady Jane' when speaking of her sister to her students. Jane always maintained that kind of status. She was very much a sophisticated lady, of the aristocracy of Alburg," and referred to as Lady Jane, especially by younger generations. Telephone conversation with David M. Bell, November 1988.

121. From a note penned onto the stockings found in the trunk in the stone tavern in Alburg, Vermont.

122. Dinsmore letter.

123. Interview with Esther Rose Rohman Price, grandmother of author: "Those dresses cost too much. I didn't buy anything I couldn't wear over and over. You didn't buy a dress for just one time; that was wasteful." June 1988, Deerfield Beach, Florida.

124. *The Art of Good Behavior,* pp. 47–51.

125. Hemenway, *Vermont Historical Gazetteer,* I, 871.

126. Calhoun, II, 34–35.

127. Crockett, pp. 64–67.

128. Carver, p. 271.

129. Carver, p. 272.

130. Carver, pp. 273–274.

131. Randall, *Mary,* p. 72.

132. Ruth Painter Randall, *The Courtship of Mr. Lincoln* (Boston: Little, Brown and Company, 1957), p. 211.

133. Randall, *Mary,* p. 74.

134. Ripley, pp. 269–270.

135. Goodwin, pp. 32–33.

136. Winifred Eliza Perkins, unpublished manuscript, "Activities at Weathersfield Center around 1864–1870," Perkins Folder at Weathersfield Historical Society, Weathersfield, Vermont.

137. Diary of Marietta Rice, March 26, 1862, from the notebooks kept by Winifred Eliza Perkins. Weathersfield Historical Society, Weathersfield, Vermont.

138. Rice diary, April 2, 1862.

139. Ethel L. Urlin, *A Short History of Marriage* (Detroit: Singing Tree Press, 1969), p. 236.

140. Rice diary, April 22, 1862.

141. Ann Monsarrat, *And the Bride Wore... The Story of the White Wedding* (New York: Dodd, Mead & Company, 1973), p. 133.

142. From *charivari,* from Late Latin *caribaria,* a headache, according to *The American Heritage Dictionary.*

143. Albert Britt, *An America That Was: What Life was Like on an Illinois Farm Seventy Years Ago* (Barre, Mass.: Barre Publishers, 1964), p. 158.

144. Joanna L. Stratton, *Pioneer Women: Voices from the Kansas Frontier* (New York: Simon and Schuster, 1982), p. 137.

145. Joe Gray Taylor, *Eating, Drinking, and Visiting in the South: An Informal History* (Baton Rouge: Louisiana State University Press, 1982), p. 48.

146. Sallie Reynolds Matthews, *Interwoven: A Pioneer Chronicle* (El Paso: Carl Hertzog, 1958), p. 23.

147. Margaret Holden Eaton, *Diary of a Sea Captain's Wife: Tales of Santa Cruz Island, 1876–1947,* ed. Janice Timbrook (Santa Barbara, Calif.: McNally & Loftin, 1983), pp. 9–10.

148. "Reminiscences: Wedding Days," from the memories of a pioneer woman in *Vermont News and Notes,* quoted in "Life Cycle."

149. Stratton, p. 136.

150. Mrs. E. L. Connally, "An Old-Time Southern Wedding," *The Sunny South,* October 31, 1903. In the subject file "Weddings," Atlanta Historical Society, Georgia.

151. Parham, p. 4H.

152. Stratton, p. 136. Daniel, the mayor of Leavenworth, Kansas, was married to Annie on January 12, 1864.

153. William C. Beecher and Samuel Scoville, assisted by Mrs. Henry Ward Beecher, *A Biography of Henry Ward Beecher* (New York: Charles L. Webster & Co., 1888), quoted in "Life Cycle."

154. Randall, *Mary,* p. 70.

155. Randall, *Courtship,* p. 206.

156. Marie D. Webster, *Quilts: Their Story and How to Make Them* (New York: Tudor Publishing Company, 1915), pp. 63–64.

157. Robertson, pp. 15–16.

158. Batchelder, p. 9.

159. Henry K. Adams, *A Centennial History of St. Albans, Vermont* (St. Albans: Wallace Printing Company, 1889), p. 93.

160. Crockett, p. 67.

161. Anita Clinton, "Stephen Arnold Douglas — His Mississippi Experience," *Journal of Mississippi History,* L, no. 2, pp. 58–59.

162. Matthews, pp. 41–42.

163. Earle, pp. 631, 634.

164. Sarah Anna Emery, *Reminiscences of a Newburyport Nonagenarian* (Newburyport, Mass.: W. H. Huse & Co., 1879), p. 47.

165. H. H. Langton, ed., *A Gentlewoman in Upper Canada: The Journals of Anne Langton* (Toronto: Clarke, Irwin, 1950), p. 24.

166. Langton, p. 127.

167. "Home and Family: Politeness Between Husband and Wife," *The Happy Home and Parlor Magazine,* V, xxxviii.

168. "The School-Mistress Married," *Godey's Lady's Book and Magazine,* XLVIII, p. 77.

169. *Bessie,* pp. 218–219.

170. Telephone interviews with Elizabeth Gillingham, granddaughter of Sarah Hoisington Richardson, Woodstock, Vermont, October, 1988.

171. Bridal album quilt, by Emily Nancy Ballard. Collection of The Charleston Museum, South Carolina.

172. Recollections of Lucinda Place Howard, as recounted by her granddaughter, Ethel Golden Nichols. From interviews at South Windham, Connecticut, 1987–1988.

173. *The Happy Home and Parlor Magazine,* VI, 133. "For a farmer, or any one that has the pleasure of eating his meals prepared by his wife or his daughters, I say give them a pleasant kitchen, where three-fourths of their time is to be spent."

174. Mary Hooker Cornelius, *The Country Kitchen 1850*, extracts from 1850 edition of *The Young Housekeeper's Friend* (Scotia, New York: Americana Review, 1965), [pages unnumbered].

175. J. Willard Reed to Stedman and Arterista Spaulding, Burke, Wisconsin, November 25, 1855. Courtesy of Barbara Chiolino.

176. David T. Nelson, trans. and ed., *The Diary of Elisabeth Koren, 1853–1855* (Northfield, Minn.: Norwegian-American Historical Association, 1955), p. 227.

177. Nannie T. Alderson and Helena Huntington Smith, *A Bride Goes West* (New York: Farrar & Rinehart, Inc., 1942), pp. 35–40.

178. Jane Tozer and Sarah Levitt, *Fabric of Society: A Century of People and their Clothes 1770–1870* (London: Laura Ashley, 1983), p. 71.

179. Conversation with Ethel Golden Nichols, South Windham, Connecticut, October 1987.

180. Alderson, pp. 14–15.

181. Conversation with Ethel Golden Nichols, South Windham, Connecticut, July 1988.

182. "Housekeeping Journal," *Godey's Lady's Book and Magazine*, LII, February 1856, p. 189.

183. Seven of Ada Taylor Dunsmoor's diaries still exist, dating from 1916 to 1925. Excerpts quoted here are from the earliest existing diary, 1916–1918. Courtesy of her grandchildren, Rebecca Merritt Garland and Henry L. Merritt.

184. Nell W. Kull, "I Can Never Be Happy There in Among So Many Mountains — The Letters of Sally Rice," *Vermont Quarterly*, XXXVIII, 50.

185. Ann Fears Crawford and Crystal Sasse Ragsdale, pp. 15–16.

186. Taylor conversation.

187. *Godey's Magazine and Lady's Book*, XLVIII, January 1854, pp. 63–64.

188. Zelotes Gates to Wm. Alfred Gates, Hartland, Vermont, April 23, 1806. Letter written in ink on leather. Courtesy of Elizabeth Graham.

189. Nelson, p. 366.

190. Ellen Spaulding Reed to her sister Leonora Spaulding Bagley, Burke, Wisconsin, October 20, 1854. Courtesy of Barbara Chiolino.

191. *The Vermont Journal*, VI, August 3, 1849.

192. *The Vermont Journal*, V, June 8, 1849.

193. Interview with Robert E. Higgins, son of Jenny Thompson Higgins, Granada Hills, California, June 9, 1988.

194. Richard G. Lillard, *The Great Forest* (New York: Alfred A. Knopf, 1947), p. 96.

195. "Cash paid out of the Estate of Thomas Place," Probate papers of Thomas Place, 1829, Book No. 17. Ashford, Windham County, Connecticut.

196. Will of Thomas Place, December 13, 1828. Ashford, Windham County, Connecticut.

197. Mansfield, p. 27.

198. "Vermont Local News, Cavendish," *Vermont Journal*, December 5, 1874, p. 4.

199. "An Impression of Eliza Prudentia Fitch by her granddaughter Winnie Perkins." Scrapbook of Winifred Eliza Perkins. Collection of the Weathersfield Historical Society, Vermont.

200. Rice diary, June 27, 1862.

201. Rice diary, September 9, 1862.

202. Rice diary, November 29, 1862.

203. Rice diary, September 9, 1862.

204. Daniel Hammond to his sons in the 12th Vermont Regiment, *Civil War Letters from Jabez H. Hammond*. Letter No. 14, unpublished manuscript. Collection of the West Windsor Historical Society, Brownsville, Vermont.

205. Carl Ubbelohde, Maxine Benson and Duane A. Smith, ed., *A Colorado Reader* (Pruett Publishing Company, 1982), pp. 12, 34.

206. United States Census 1900, Denver City, Arapahoe County, Colorado, June 5, 1900. Cora A. Higgins is listed as "servant" for Charles H. Toll and his wife and four sons.

207. George Elliott Howard, *A History of Matrimonial Institutions* (New York: Humanities Press, 1964), III, 156.

208. Harriet Fisher Higgins to granddaughter Lucy J. Higgins, Hinsdale, New Hampshire, May 24, 1914. Courtesy of Robert E. Higgins.

209. Hastings conversation.

210. Perkins, p. 123.

211. Hastings conversation.

212. Perkins, [page unnumbered].

213. Ellen Spaulding Reed to Arterista and Stedman Spaulding, Burke, Wisconsin, October 27, 1854.

214. "The Five Weddings," *Godey's Lady's Book and Magazine*, LXXV, December 1867, p. 548.

215. "Hartland," *Vermont Journal*, XXXI, January 29, 1876.

216. Mary Beardsley Fenn, *Parish and Town: The History of West Windsor, Vermont* (Taftsville, Vermont: The Countryman Press, 1977), p. 145.

217. Diary of Ada Taylor Dunsmoor, 1923, West Windsor, Vermont. Courtesy of grandchildren Rebecca Merritt Garland and Henry L. Merritt.

218. Alva Dunsmoor to daughter-in-law Martha Dunsmoor, Windsor, Vermont, March 4, 1927. Courtesy of grandson John A. Dunsmoor.

219. *Massachusetts Journal & Tribune*, VI, no. 11, Boston, November 5, 1831, [p. 3].

220. *Massachusetts Journal & Tribune*, V, no. 28, Boston, March 5, 1831, [p. 3].

PATTERNS AND INSTRUCTIONS FOR THREE ANTIQUE BRIDAL FRIENDSHIP QUILTS

GENERAL INSTRUCTIONS

SUPPLIES
template plastic
ultra-fine permanent pen
artist's soft pencil (white, gray or silver)
scissors
glass-head pins
cotton thread
hand-sewing needle for traditional piecing *or*
rotary cutter, wide plastic ruler, cutting board and sewing machine for quick cutting and piecing
iron
light-colored towel
pressing surface
batting
quilting thread
quilting needle (Between)
thimble
quilting hoop or frame

Yardage and instructions are given for the quilts as they were made. For example, the *Chimney Sweep* has a border on only one side and the *Texas Star* has borders on three sides only.

1. Choose the pattern you desire to make. Complete yardage and cutting charts are given for three sizes: crib/wall, twin and double/queen. Each pattern includes a diagram indicating the required templates. Cutting instructions are given for traditional cutting (using the templates) or quick-cutting methods.

2. If you will be using traditional methods, use the permanent pen to trace the appropriate templates onto the template plastic. Cut the individual templates apart using your scissors or a rotary cutter with wide plastic ruler and cutting board. Indicate the letter and the direction of the grainline on each template.

3. Lay the template on the *wrong* side of the fabric and, using your artist's pencil, trace around each template, making sure the grainline on the template corresponds to that of the fabric.

4. Cut out the fabric pieces using either a rotary cutter with a wide plastic ruler and cutting board or fabric scissors.

5. If you will be using quick-cutting methods, use your rotary cutter with a wide plastic ruler and cutting board to cut the appropriate number of fabric strips as indicated in the cutting charts.

6. Using either your sewing machine or hand-sewing needle, construct the individual blocks according to the diagrams, using a 1/4" seam allowance.

7. For best results, it is recommended to press as you sew. The light-colored towel placed on your pressing surface makes a good padding. Whenever possible, press the seams in the direction of the darker fabric. After you have sewn a seam, press the fabrics flat to set the stitches in place. Then, fold the top piece of fabric back over the stitching line. Press again. *Do not iron*, just press.

8. Give each completed block a final pressing on its right side.

9. Join the blocks in either a diagonal set or straight set, as indicated by each pattern.

10. Give the quilt top a final pressing on its *right* side.

11. Use the artist's pencil to mark any desired quilting lines lightly onto the quilt top.

12. To prepare the backing, cut the backing fabric into the required number of lengths. Cut off the selvages. Sew the pieces together lengthwise with a 1/4" seam. Press the seam(s) to one direction. The backing should measure *at least* 2" larger than the quilt top all the way around.

13. If you will be quilting in a hoop, layer the backing, batting (cut 1/2"

larger than the quilt top all the way around) and the quilt top. Baste the three layers together with a long diagonal basting stitch.

14. Fold the excess 2″ of backing in half and then in half again, bringing the folded edge of the backing even with the edge of the quilt top. Pin. Hand baste in place all the way around. This will protect the edge of the quilt top.

15. Using a quilting hoop and starting in the center of the quilt, quilt through all three layers with small running stitches.

Or, if you will be using a frame, follow the instructions which accompany your frame.

16. Trim the excess backing and batting, and straighten the edges if they have stretched during quilting.

17. Attach the binding. The quilts are finished with a narrow 1/4″ binding. Cut strips of fabric 1¾″ wide and sew them together end to end to form one continuous strip. With the right side on the outside, fold the strip in half lengthwise and sew it to the right side of the quilt with a 1/4″ seam. Turn the binding to the back side of the quilt and hand slip stitch in place.

If you are a beginner or are unfamiliar with the basic techniques described above, detailed instructions on cutting, piecing and quilting can be found in *Quilts! Quilts!! Quilts!!! — The Complete Guide to Quiltmaking* by Diana McClun and Laura Nownes, also published by The Quilt Digest Press. This is an excellent resource book for anyone wanting to make an heirloom quilt. It is a worthwhile investment.

HARRIET FISHER HIGGINS'S "ALBUM PATCH" QUILT

(shown on page 100)

	Wall/Crib	Twin	Double/Queen
Finished size	53″×62″	71″×97″	88″×97″
Blocks set	3×3	4×5	5×5
Number of whole blocks	15	35	45
Number of half blocks	2	3	4
Number of quarter blocks	2	2	2
Number of side triangles	9	14	15
YARDAGE			
Muslin	1	1½	1¾
Prints: scraps to total	2¼	5	5½
Side triangles	⅞	⅞	⅞
Sashing and binding	2	3	3½
Backing	3½	6¼	8
CUTTING			
Muslin:			
Template A	15	35	45
— OR —			
Quick: number of strips	2	3	4
Template D	2	3	4
— OR —			
Quick: number of strips	(Use remainder of Template A strip)		

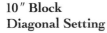

**10″ Block
Diagonal Setting**

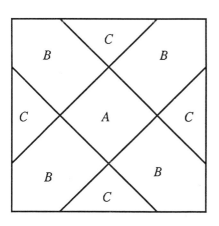

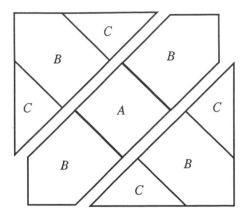

Template F	2	2	2
— OR —			
Quick: number of strips	1	1	1
Template G (posts)	15	35	45
— OR —			
Quick: number of strips	2	3	4
Template J (side post triangle)	11	17	19
— OR —			
Quick: number of strips	1	1	1
Template K (bottom corner post triangle)	2	2	2
— OR —			
Quick: number of strips	1	1	1
Prints:			
Template B	62	143	184
Template C	66	148	190
— OR —			
Quick: number of strips	4	8	10
Template E	4 & 4r°	5 & 5r	6 & 6r
Sashing:			
Quick: number of lengthwise strips	7	9	10
Side triangles: number of 15″ squares	3	4	4
Backing: number of lengths	2	2	3

°r = reverse template on fabric.

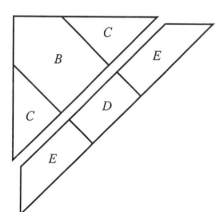

Instructions for quick cutting (cut all fabrics crossgrain):

For Template A: Cut 3⅜″-wide strips, then cut to 3⅜″ squares.

For Template C: Cut 7¼″-wide strips, then cut to 7¼″ squares. Cut each square into *quarters diagonally*.

For Template D: Cut 3⅜″-wide strips, then cut to 1¹⁵⁄₁₆″ (just shy of 2″) × 3⅜″ rectangles.

For Template F: Cut 1¹⁵⁄₁₆″ (just shy of 2″)-wide strips, then cut to 1¹⁵⁄₁₆″ squares.

For Template G: Cut 3″-wide strips, then cut to 3″ squares.

For sashing: Cut 3″-wide strips × the length of your sashing fabric, then cut the lengths to 3″ × 10½″ rectangles.

For Template J: Cut 4¾″-wide strips, then cut to 4¾″ squares. Cut each square into *quarters diagonally*.

For Template K: Cut 2½″-wide strips, then cut to 2½″ squares. Cut each square in *half diagonally*.

For side triangles: Cut each square into *quarters diagonally*. Cutting side triangles in this manner will allow for a straight grain of fabric around the entire outer edge of the quilt. The triangles will be a little "too big" but can be trimmed after the blocks are sewn together.

For Templates B and E: Use traditional methods. For help, see steps 2–4 of the General Instructions.

CONSTRUCTION

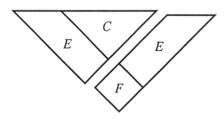

1. Construct the required number of whole blocks, referring to the diagram.

2. Construct the required number of half blocks, referring to the diagram.

3. Construct two quarter blocks (for the top corners), referring to the diagram.

4. Lay all of the whole blocks, half blocks, quarter blocks, sashing strips, posts and quarter triangles on the floor in their proper sequence. Refer to the color photograph shown on page 100 for help.

5. Sew the blocks together in a diagonal set. Join them to the sashing strips and posts.

6. Proceed with preparing the backing, quilting and attaching the binding as directed in the General Instructions.

ADA CADY TAYLOR DUNSMOOR'S "TEXAS STAR" QUILT

(shown on page 96)

	Wall/Crib	Twin	Double/Queen
Finished size	47″ × 56″	68″ × 88″	89″ × 98″
Blocks set	4 × 5	6 × 8	8 × 9
Total number of blocks	20	48	72
YARDAGE			
Muslin	2	4¼	6¼
Prints: scraps to total	1½	3	4½
Borders and binding	1¾	2⅝	3
Backing	3	6	8
CUTTING			
Muslin:			
Template Q	20	48	72
Template S	40 & 40r*	96 & 96r	144 & 144r
Template T	40	96	144
Prints:			
Template R	120	288	432
Borders:			
Two 3″ strips (for sides), *each*	54″	85″	96″
One 4″ strip (for end)	49″	70″	90″
Backing: number of lengths	2	3	3

r = reverse template on fabric.

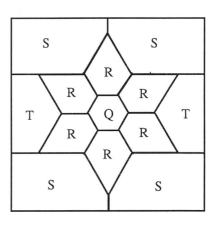

**10½″ Block
Straight Setting**

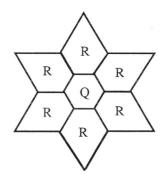

To achieve accuracy in construction it is recommended that this pattern be hand pieced. Remember that in hand piecing the stitches must not extend into the seam allowance.

CONSTRUCTION

1. Construct the required number of blocks, referring to the diagram. The star points (Template R) are joined first and then the center (Template Q) is inset. Since you will be hand piecing, when joining Template Q you can simply take a small backstitch at the end of each stitching line, flip the seam joining two Template R's to one side and continue stitching around the next side of Template Q. This will complete one star unit as shown in the diagram.

2. Attach two Template T's to opposite sides of the star unit as shown in the diagram.

3. Attach four Template S's (remember that two were cut reversed) to the previously sewn unit, as shown in the diagram.

4. Sew all of the blocks together in a straight set.

5. Attach borders to three sides only.

6. Proceed with preparing the backing, quilting and attaching the binding as directed in the General Instructions.

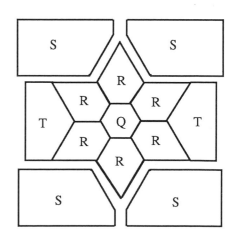

8½″ Block
Diagonal Setting

	Wall/Crib	Twin	Double/Queen
Finished size	48″×64″	78″×94″	93″×94″
Blocks set	3×4	5×6	6×6
Total number of blocks	18	50	61
Number of large side triangles (for top and sides)	8	14	15
Number of small side triangles (for bottom)	2	4	5
Number of large corner triangles	2	2	2
Number of small corner triangles	2	2	2

YARDAGE

Muslin	1¼	2½	3
Prints: scraps to total	1¼	2¾	3¼
Sashing, border and top binding	2½	3½	3⅝
Side triangles and side and bottom binding	2	2⅝	2⅝
Backing	4	5¾	8½

CUTTING

Muslin:			
Template L	36	100	122
— OR —			
Quick: number of strips	2	5	6
Template M	18	50	61
— OR —			
Quick: number of strips	1	3	3
Template N	216	600	732
— OR —			
Quick: number of strips	5	13	16
Template P	72	200	244
— OR —			
Quick: number of strips	2	5	6
Prints:			
Template L	144	400	488
— OR —			
Quick: number of strips	7	20	24
Template M	72	200	244
— OR —			
Quick: number of strips	4	10	12
Border: cut one 4½″ strip (for top only)	49″	79″	94″
Sashing:	Cut strips 2¾″ wide × length of fabric.		
Side and corner triangles:			
Large side triangles: number of 17″ squares	2	4	4
Small side triangles: number of 11″ squares	1	1	2
Large corner triangles: number of 10″ squares	1	1	1

Small corner triangles: **number of 6½″ squares**	1	1	1
Backing: number of lengths	2	2	3

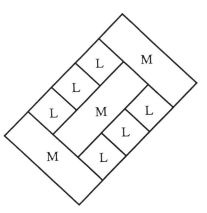

Instructions for quick cutting (cut all fabrics, except sashing and borders, cross-grain):

For Template L: Cut 2″-wide strips, then cut to 2″ squares.

For Template M: Cut 5″-wide strips, then cut to 2″ × 5″ rectangles.

For Template N: Cut 3⅜″-wide strips, then cut to 3⅜″ squares. Cut each square into *quarters diagonally.*

For Template P: Cut 1 15/16″ (just shy of 2″)-wide strips, then cut to 1 15/16″ squares. Cut each square in *half diagonally.*

For large side triangles: Cut each square into *quarters diagonally.*

For small side triangles: Cut each square into *quarters diagonally.*

For large corner triangles: Cut the square in *half diagonally.*

For small corner triangles: Cut the square in *half diagonally.*

Cutting side triangles in this manner will allow for a straight grain of fabric around the entire outer edge of the quilt. The triangles will be a little "too big," but can be trimmed after the blocks are sewn together.

CONSTRUCTION

1. Construct the required number of blocks, referring to the diagrams.

2. Lay all of the blocks, side triangles and sashing strips on the floor in their proper sequence.

3. Sew the blocks together in a diagonal set. Join them to the sashing strips.

4. Attach the border to one side only, as shown in the photograph on page 93.

5. Proceed with preparing the backing, quilting and attaching the binding as directed in the General Instructions.

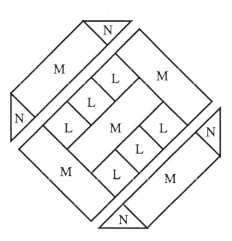

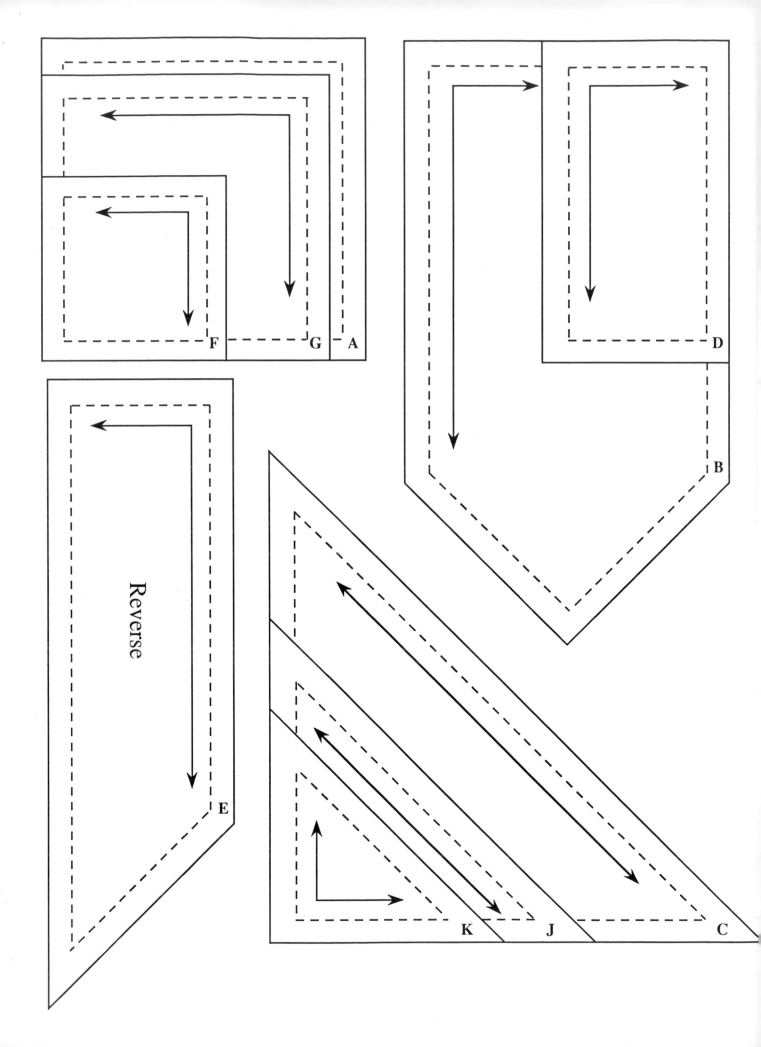

A

B

C

D

E

Reverse

F

G

J

K

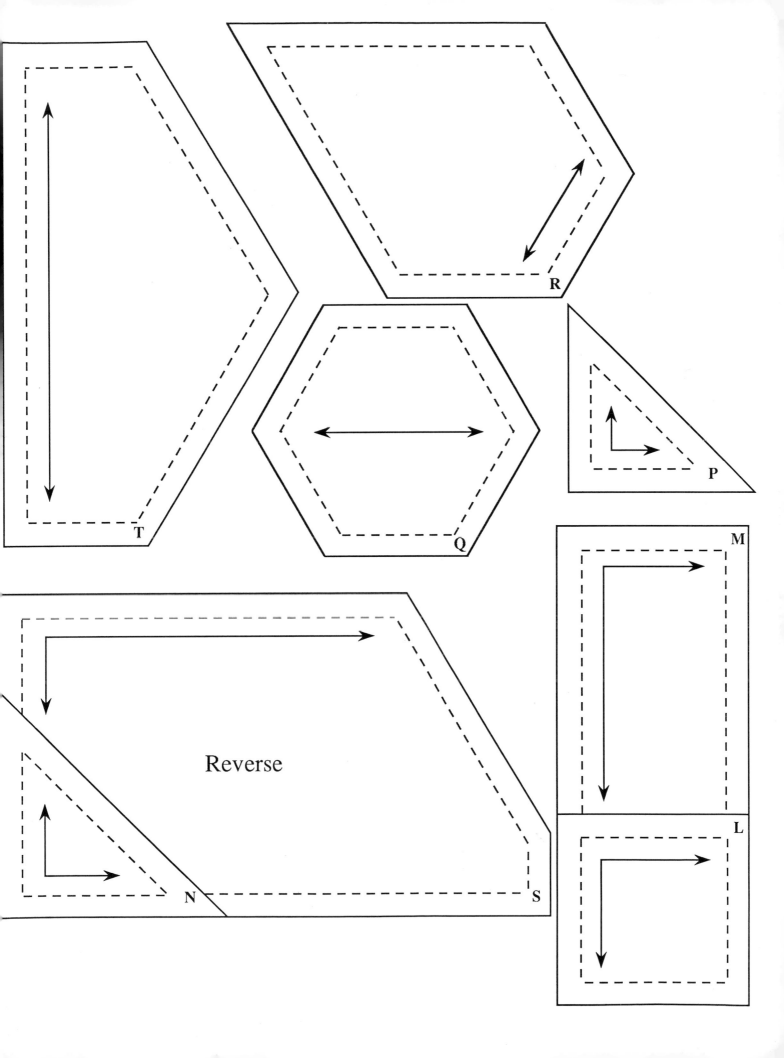

T

R

Q

P

Reverse

N

S

M

L

Simply the Best

*W*hen we started our publishing efforts in 1983, we made one pledge to ourselves: to produce the finest quilt books imaginable. The critics and our loyal readers clearly believe that we're living up to that promise.

In a time when thin, 64-page quilt books with only staples to hold their pages intact and small numbers of color photos sell for as much as $19.95, we are proud that our books set a noticeably higher standard.

Books from The Quilt Digest Press are hefty, with many more pages and masses of color photos. They are printed on high-quality satin-finish paper and are bound with durable glues and spines to last a lifetime. The world's finest quilt photographer does all our work. A great design team lavishes its attention on every detail of every page. And the world's finest commercial printer sees to it that every book is a gem. Add knowledgeable authors with vital ideas and you, too, will say, "The Quilt Digest Press? Oh, they're Simply the Best."

Try another of our books. They're as good as the one in your hands. And write for our free 12-page color catalogue.

THE QUILT DIGEST PRESS

Dept. D
955 Fourteenth Street
San Francisco 94114